THE FRUITS OF WORSHIP

THE FRUITS OF WORSHIP

Abdullah Aymaz

New Jersey

Copyright © 2011 by Tughra Books
Copyright © 2011 by Işık Yayınları

Originally published in Turkish as *İbadetin Getirdikleri* in 2003
14 13 12 11   1 2 3 4

All rights reserved. No part of this book may be reproduced or transmitted
in any form or by any means, electronic or mechanical, including pho-
tocopying, recording or by any information storage and retrieval system
without permission in writing from the Publisher.

Published by Tughra Books
345 Clifton Ave., Clifton,
NJ, 07011, USA

www.tughrabooks.com

Library of Congress Cataloging-in-Publication Data Available

Translated by Ömer A. Ergi

ISBN: 978-1-59784-252-5

Printed by
İmak Ofset Basım Yayın Istanbul-TURKEY

CONTENTS

CHAPTER I

Worship and the Obligatory Daily Prayers

Human beings are created in the best of molds and distinguished from all of God's other creations. For this reason, they prefer a lifestyle that is worthy of a human being. This is quite evident in their selection of clothes and living standards. As a result of their superiority over the rest of God's creation, they constantly seek beauty, ask for the best and wish to live honorable lives. However, these objectives cannot be obtained in a life of solitude. Perhaps, a life of solitude is possible for the members of the animal kingdom. The reason for this is the fact that their clothes are provided at birth and since their senses for taste is limited, they do not require a large variety of food. Moreover, animals do not possess the necessary intelligence to develop passion for science, research, and arts, so these issues do not concern them. Whereas, human beings need knowledge, art, and trade to survive. Therefore, in order to survive, human beings need each other. This means that human beings were created civilized in their natural disposition. They are compelled to live in communities. It is through this social life they are able to obtain their needs and necessities. They utilize the profits they obtain in an exchange process to support each other's requirements.

On the other hand, human beings are equipped with certain disproportionate emotions and essentials such as passion, wrath, and intelligence. Various levels of these fundamental human essentials form different characters such as tough, weak, cunning, understanding, ignorant, etc… Thus human societies are made up of many different characters and personalities. This in turn creates a medium for unjust behavior, human rights violations, and mistreatment of others. In order to prevent such violations, human societies need justice. Justice can only be imposed through a legal system.

However, no matter how perfect a legal system is, it has no value unless it is implemented. Quite often, feelings such as greed, personal interest, selfishness, rancor, and revenge can push human beings into breaking the law. This means we need a control system where human beings can be protected from evil even in places or situations where the legal system cannot apprehend or deal with evildoers. Since we cannot assign a police officer to every citizen in the society, we need to place the fear of God into the hearts of every human being. Human beings need to understand that on the Day of Judgment, God will hold them accountable for every deed they have committed on earth. Righteous deeds will certainly be rewarded, and there will most certainly be punishment for evil acts. Such concepts can only be embraced and developed through the principles of faith, especially faith in God and in Judgment Day. This most imperative faith can only be renewed and rejuvenated through the daily prayers. The reason for this is that worship is the only thing that strengthens the faith and converts it into a habitual veracity. Without doubt, if principles of faith are not supported and maintained with practice and worship, which consists of obeying God and refraining from what He has forbidden, faith will constantly be weakened. The biggest evidence of this is the current situation of the world of Islam.

a. Human Beings and Solving
the Enigma of Creation

The purpose of worship is to remember God. Turning towards God will result in obedience and submission. Moreover, submitting to God and obeying His commandments of Divine Wisdom will bring order and perfection to humanity. It is only through human perfection and order that the divine purpose behind the creation of the universe will prevail. The reason behind the apparent beauty in the universe is the obedience and submission displayed by all matter. Certainly, all creation from the tiniest grains to the stars in the Heavens praises and glorifies God: *"The armies of the earth and heavens above belong to God"* (Fath 48:4), and *"Small and big, everything glorifies God"* (Isra 17:44). These inanimate beings display their inner beauty and amazing ability which was created by God through their obedience to God. If they were not part of God's supreme plan, the apparent beauty observed in the universe would not exist. On the other hand, thousands of mysteries in relation to God's divine wisdom are concealed in the human soul. These hidden treasures and capabilities can only be revealed and developed through obedience and submission to God.

God has created the human being as an index which contains the great book of the entire universe. And He has implanted a sample from each of His Beautiful Names that reflect on all worlds and realms into the quintessence of humanity. If human beings utilize these treasures by using their physical organs and spiritual senses in obedience and worship of God, those samples implanted in their quintessence will transform into metaphysical windows through which the corresponding realm would be observed. Moreover, they would assume the role of a mirror reflecting the Divine Name that manifests in that particular realm. Consequently, the body and soul of these individuals will become an abstract of both the physical and metaphysical worlds. As a result, the Divine Names that manifest in both worlds will also be reflected by their souls. In this regard, human beings become the receptors and reflectors of Divine Names. For this reason, great Islamic scholar, Muhyiddin ibn al-Arabi interprets the hadith qudsi, "I was a Hidden Treasure. I have created the living beings so that they may discover Me," as "I have created living beings as mirrors so I may observe the reflection of My Beauty in them."

b. Center of Attraction

Human beings are the central point of creation. Rays emitted by laws of nature, universal principles, and precise measurements of existence are all composed in the essence of human beings. Therefore, in order to achieve the smooth flow of this universal current, human beings need to comply with these laws and principles. It is imperative that human beings perform the duties appointed by God, in order to avoid the possibility of being crushed under the pallets of the immense system that functions throughout the universe. The reason for this is the fact that the order and harmony that is apparent in the universe originates from the total submission shown to the Divine plan. Likewise, the evident beauty observed in all matter, from atoms to galaxies, derives from the reflections of Divine Names that organizes and decorates them. The mysteries embedded in the human soul will also be revealed and manifested through obedience and submission to the Divine decree which is distributed through the reflections of His Beautiful Names. Without doubt, through submission and obedience human capabilities will develop and flourish. In contrast, just as those who lose their arms and legs by disobeying the rules of machinery usage, those who disobey the Divine principles will gradually lose their physical and spiritual senses and emotions. Certainly, the universe was established on order, harmony, and obedience.

c. Many Responsibilities

By obeying God's commandments and refraining from what He has forbidden, a human being becomes involved in many aspects of social life. Particularly, in relation to religious principles and matters that are beneficial to society, one individual represents the entire human race. Since Muslims need to fulfill their obligations towards God, they need to undertake many different tasks such as religious duties, social responsibilities, instructing duties, community development, and rehabilitation. Therefore, they need to carry many sensitive issues such as justice and social integrity on their shoulders.

If there is no one to undertake these duties and obligations, they will be stepped on by everyone.

d. Brotherhood and Ascension

By means of belief in Islam and worship, human beings develop strong bonds with all believers. For example, in the army, close friendships are established by serving under the same commander; this feeling of friendship is further strengthened by serving in the same platoon. Moreover, being from the same town develops a sense of brotherhood between the soldiers. Just as the example, believing in the same God, performing the same form of worship, following the same Prophet, turning towards the same *qiblah*, or direction of prayer, and hence being the member of the same religion enables the development of a strong bond of friendship and solid feeling of brotherhood amongst believers. These significant religious bonds do not bring together only humankind, but they are like metaphysical chains that establish a bond between all of creation. Such powerful bond and brotherhood give birth to everlasting love. Essentially, social cohesion and harmony can only be obtained through love, mutual respect, and brotherhood.

e. Maturity and Personal Development Can Be Achieved through Worship

From a physical perspective, human beings are quite tiny, feeble, and insignificant. They are considered to be one of the many species of mammals that inhabit the earth. However, human beings possess exalted souls and a potential to achieve great things. They have countless inclinations, never ending requests and desires. Moreover, human beings have unlimited ideas and unrestricted emotions such, as passion and wrath. Consequently, they were created with an essence that holds the contents of all living species. The exalted soul of such being can only be satisfied with worship; only worship can develop their abilities, and only worship can protect them from evil temptations and carnal desires. It is also through worship that the interminable desires of human beings can be fulfilled. Worship also plays the role of a daily-coordinator that brings order to one's life. Worship cleans and purifies the inner and exterior organs of human beings from the stains and blemishes left behind by nature. It ascends the human soul and brings it to the proximity of God.

Man can reach the utmost nearness with the Almighty through performing his duties of servanthood, the prescribed daily prayers in particular. Standing before God five times a day, the believer forms the most powerful and the most beautiful bond with his Lord. It is through the prayers (*salah*) that the believer connects his infinite weakness to the infinite power of God and becomes closer to the Almighty. This is why God's Messenger said, "Prayer is the Ascension of a believer (to God's proximity)." Again in the words of the Prophet, "The prayer is the main pillar of the religion." For this reason, Islam is more particular regarding the establishment of this main pillar of religion than any other form of worship. Indeed, it is an uncompromising condition of being a devout believer and the most important duty of servanthood following faith.

THE IMPACT OF FAITH ON SOCIETY AND INDIVIDUALS

There is a profound connection between faith and human beings. In his book, entitled *Return to Religion*, Dr. Henry Link evaluates the results of research that included 73,226 psychological experiments conducted on 15,321 male and female subjects in the USA: "Individuals who believe in a religion and attend to the services provided by their place of worship on regular basis have strong and consistent personalities and possess a superior character to those who neglect faith and worship."

In his book, *How to Stop Worrying and Start Living*, Dale Carnegie offers the following advice for the prevention of distress: "Today I shall allocate half an hour to respite and during this period I will think of God."

William James, a Professor of Philosophy from Harvard University states, "Religion is the strongest medicine for reservations." In addition, Dr. A. A. Brill claims that a truly pious individual will not suffer from psychological disorders.

Psychologists have established that strong faith and regular prayers prevent the development of needless worries, unsubstantiated fear, and depression. These are the psychological problems which give birth to half of human illnesses and health disorders.

In *Modern Man in Search of Soul*, Dr. Carl Jung, one of the most prominent psychiatrists of our time, explains, "During the last thirty years of my practice, I have examined hundreds of patients from all over the world. Those who were over the age of thirty-five had a common problem. Their illnesses were triggered by loss of faith. Their perspective on life had changed. Unlike their pious friends, they were not behaving in a faithful manner. These patients would not totally recover until they re-embraced their faith."

The great Indian leader, Mahatma Gandhi stated, "If it was not for the prayers, I would have lost my mind within a short period of time."

In an article that appeared in *Reader's Digest*, Nobel laureate Dr. Alexis Carrel states, "Prayer is the most powerful action that a person can take. Prayer is an authentic force, just like earth's gravity. Through the power of prayer, I have witnessed the recovery of many patients who did not respond to conventional medical treatments."

Psychiatrists tell us that talking to someone about our problems during times of depression and stress is the best medicine. When we pray, we have the opportunity to talk to God about all of our problems, even those that we cannot reveal to others. Consequently, we can ask for His aid and beseech His support in a direct manner.

In his book, entitled *Pascal*, Jacques Chevalier refers to Pascal's statement about God, "Those who fail to search for God or turn away from Him will never find the truth or true happiness whether he seeks it internally or externally."

Faith also plays a great role in strengthening the bonds between family members. In his work entitled, *Divorce*, J. Dominian cites, "Marriages performed through religious ceremonies are less likely to end with divorce than the others." In the same book, he emphasizes that statistically, the divorce rate in non-religious marriages is quite high.

Lack of faith also plays a significant role in suicides. Those who believe that materialistic wealth solves all problems will be shocked by the statistics conducted in wealthy nations.

For example, Japan's suicide rate is among the highest in the industrialized world. The statistics of the Japanese National Police Agency state that the number in 2003 reached 34,427, and this is equivalent of 27 per 100 thousand citizens. In the US, 32,439 suicides occurred in 2004, and this is equivalent of 86 suicides per day or one suicide every 16 minutes. Each year over one hundred doctors commit suicide in the US alone. According to a recent report from the World Health Organization, the highest rates of suicide are seen in the former communist-dominated societies followed by the advanced western countries while the lowest rates are found in more religious societies, such as Latin American and Muslim countries. Those who base everything on materialism and believe that a strong economy is the only infrastructure of a happy life should stop to think for a moment. Let us not forget the fact that these nations mentioned above have achieved a high standard in socio-economics, education, and culture.

It is obvious that Freud and Adler were wrong in their claims. Without question, these nations have strong economies, and they provide sexual freedom for their citizens. Then what is the reason beyond so many suicides?

Whereas Egypt is a much poorer nation than those mentioned above, yet the suicide rate in Egypt is five in ten million. In Switzerland and France, this rate is seventeen in hundred thousand. As it is quite perceptible, solving the financial issues of a nation is not enough to bring happiness to its people. Here are a number of examples from some nations that build their civilization on material wealth:

From 1960 to 1970 there was a 144% increase in serious crimes in the USA. Despite the steady development in economic conditions in the US, the Uniform Crime Report indicates that between 1960 and 1975 reported rates of aggravated assault, forcible rape, and homicide increased by 164%, 174%, and 188%, respectively. Between 1955 and 1965 there was approximately a 200% increase in the USA in burglary and theft, and a 100% increase in nations such as France, Italy, Norway and UK. Over the period 1997-2009, violent attacks increased by 77% in the UK. In 2007 alone, approximately one and a half million people were victims of violent crime in the US.

According to crime statistics, the percentage of hardened criminals in the nations below is as follows: 78.5% of every thousand citizens have committed serious crimes in Sweden. These numbers are 64.5% in Denmark; 44.2% in Germany; 41.2% in USA; 34.6 in France. 1,827, 373 criminal offences were committed in France in a single year (1974). There was a 6.57% increase in burglary, theft, fraud, and money laundering in 1973. The rate of these crimes had increased by 12.07% in 1974. According to statistics, there were 2,700 burglaries taking place each day in France throughout 1972. This number had increased to 3,081 in 1973. The recent data also show that violent crime and robbery have been rising in European countries. For the EU member states, the violent crime was up 3% and robbery up 1% in the period 1998-2007. The prison population rose by about 1% annually over 1998-2007 to reach an average rate in EU member states of 123 prisoners per hundred thousand citizens for the years 2005-2007. The percentage of crimes in youth is also increasing dramatically. According to the US Justice department, one-third of all victims of violent crime were teenagers ages

12-19, and 50% of all violent crimes were committed by young people in 1998.

In his book called, *La Revaite Contre La Pere*, Geruva Mendel states, "Rebellion against the father transforms into feelings of revenge against all authority figures." Good conduct can be best acquired and practiced in the family. Indeed, the respect and reverence shown by parents to their own mother and father (i.e. the children's grandparents) serve as a great lesson to the youth. If a child's mother and father are always loving and compassionate, the child will be more aware of the duty and obligation to respect their parents and other elders. People develop this awareness over a long time and through habit. In addition, Islam forbids its followers from saying even a simple word of contempt to ones parents:

> Your Lord has decreed that you worship none but Him alone, and treat parents with the best of kindness. Should one of them, or both, attain old age in your lifetime, do not say "Ugh!" to them (as an indication of complaint or impatience), nor push them away, and always address them in gracious words. Lower to them the wing of humility out of mercy, and say: "My Lord, have mercy on them even as they cared for me in childhood." (Isra, 17:23–24)

The power of religion in relation to kicking bad habits is also quite evident. During the prohibition of alcohol in the USA from 1930-1933, the government spent two million dollars on printed propaganda materials alone. Five hundred thousand people were convicted and two hundred people were killed in three years of prohibition; yet still, alcohol could not be cleared off the streets.

Conventional methods of treating alcoholics are not really working. Today, psychiatrists are vigorously working on new treatments for alcoholism. Unfortunately, most alcoholics who go through the rehabilitation program go back to drinking within a short period of a few months. On the other hand, fourteen centuries ago, Prophet Muhammad, peace and blessings be upon him, abolished the consumption of alcohol from his society of strong believers using the method of gradualism in accordance with the coming Revelations. As is known, the verses of Qur'an were not sent down to the Prophet all at one time. Since people were indulging in all their misguided customs and behaviors that existed before the advent of the Revelations and they were not inclined to abandon such bad habits at once, the process of giving up alcohol was completed through three stages. The Prophet succeeded in cleaning hundreds of bad habits from his society with great ease, gradually, but within a very short period of time. Aisha, the wife of the Prophet, tells us that in the early days of Islam verses that sought to change a person's heart and mind were revealed, and later the verses that laid down divine law were sent. She says, "People would have said 'We shall never give up alcohol' if the command 'Do not drink alcohol' had been revealed in the beginning" thus clearly explaining the rationale behind this method of gradual change in society.

There is an organization in New York established to help people quit drinking. When this organization was first established, its members decided to conduct a historical research to find out the first incident of alcohol prohibition. They found that the first alcohol prohibition was implemented by the Prophet of Islam. Following the discovery, some members of the organization proposed that a monument be built to commemorate Muhammad, peace and blessings be upon him. One member suggested that a statue of the Prophet be made. Another member argued against this by saying, "The followers of this religion would prefer the construction of something from which the society would benefit." Since the second proposal seemed more appropriate to the teachings of Islam and Muhammad, the organization decided to make a water fountain in the name of the noble Prophet. The fountain was constructed in New York and given the title of "Muhammad's Tap." Soon after, Malik ibn Suud was selected as the chairman of the organization.

Today, humanity is going through a period of depression triggered by a lack of faith. Religion prescribes the protection of five imperative essentials:

1. Protection of health
2. Protection of sanity
3. Protection of property
4. Protection of human dignity and decorum
5. Protection of religion itself

Indeed, those who have distanced themselves from religion have sought refuge in substances like alcohol and illegal drugs.

In *The Matter of Hashish and Turkey*, Prof. Ayhan Songar provides some statistical information about heroin addicts in the US:

In 1972 there were 600,000 heroin addicts in the US,

In 1973 this number climbed to 612,000 and,

In 1974 there were 650,000 addicts.

More than 6 million people have applied for rehabilitation and 55 million people thought to have used some form of synthetic drug. Why do such large numbers of Americans resort to drugs when they live in one of the wealthiest nations on earth?

These addictions also have serious impact on family life. Here is the demographical chart of some civilized nations released by United Nations in 1974:

Country	Marriage Rate	Divorce Rate
Denmark	6.11	2.5
Sweden	5.5	3.1
UK	8.1	2.0
USA	10.1	4.6
Russia	10.1	2.7
Germany	6.1	1.4

According to Dr. Sarroks, 40% of American wives live in separation from their husbands, and this costs the US economy 250 million additional dollars each year.

Another issue that religion emphasizes is the institution of marriage. It is common knowledge that most sexually transmitted diseases arise from out-of-marriage relationships. According to Britannica, since the number of marriages has fallen drastically in the US, hospitals have treated over 360,000 patients who complained from sexually transmitted diseases. Currently, there are 65 major hospitals specialized in treating these type of diseases in the US alone.

In America, each year 30 to 40 thousand children die from sexually transmitted diseases that pass through genetics. Records suggest that 61% of Americans have complained about some form of sexual disorder. These diseases have been diagnosed in both married and single individuals. According to gynecologists, 7% percent of American women who had vaginal surgeries developed the problem due to some form of sexually transmitted disease.

Some sexually transmitted diseases can cause many other complications in the body. These complications can vary from brain paralysis, stomach problems, intestine disorders, bone ailments, and aorta complications. During the first two years of the WWI, 75,000 French soldiers suffered from sexually transmitted diseases. According to historical records, one small regiment had 242 cases of the very same disease.

According to Michael Frayn, who writes in the Observer, Switzerland has the highest rate of alcoholism, crime, abortion, traffic accidents, out of marriage relations, and suicide.

In Sweden, the number of teenagers with alcohol abuse problem has tripled during the last 15 years. Today, 50% of Swedish teenagers are going through some form of depression. US authorities have admitted that 6 out of 7 youths in America are not fit for military duty due to inappropriate behavior or character disorders.

Those who do not value the important ethical principles of religion, such as, decency, chastity, and integrity should lend their ears to Dr. Alexis Carrel, one of the great minds of the twentieth century, who said: "Intellect with its powerful faculties can only manifest through the temporary control of sexual desires and the appropriate development of gender glands."

People at mature age, especially the younger generation, should carefully listen to the following advice:

"Without doubt, one day your youth will abandon you. Just as summer makes way for autumn and it too makes way for winter, youth will leave its place to old age, and old age will leave its place to death. The holy Qur'an and all the divine decrees clearly indicate that if one spends his temporary youth with decency and on the path of righteousness, he will be rewarded with eternal youth. If it is wasted on evil and indecency, it will bring despair and suffering, just as a murder committed with a minute of rage entails years of suffering in prison. Not only will the licentious desires and pleasures of youth cause accountability on the Day of Judgment, suffering in the grave, and despair on earth, but it will bring pain within the pleasure itself, and this pain will be more than the pleasure. Any young person who has common sense will confirm this. For example, within an indecent desire there is despair of rejection, misery of jealousy, and anguish of separation that co-exists with a small amount of pleasure which makes the whole thing seem like a poisonous honey. If you wish to know the results of wasting your youth on evil deeds just ask the bars, hospitals, prisons, and cemeteries that are full of young people. Many have ended up in hospitals due to indecent behavior; many have been incarcerated due to unlawful acts. There are those who seek refuge in bars due to spiritual disorders originating from lack of obedience and spiritualism and those who have ended up in the grave because of rebellious behavior."

Due to the increasing rate of divorce in the USA, out of 45 million children who belong to broken families, 12 million are left without parents. No doubt, these children who have no families will eventually grow up to be nuisance to the society. Children born from out of marriage relations have the greatest risk of developing psychological disorders.

The suicide rate in the UK is 16 people per day or approximately 6,000 a year. In the United States, this number is 86 suicides per day. This means that someone commits or attempts to commit suicide every sixteen minutes. Let us not forget the fact that all incidents of suicide attempts are not reported to the authorities. Some claim that in order to reflect the real numbers, the ratio have to be lifted by 30%.

In the UK, during the last 60 years, the number of male suicides has risen by 31%. This number is more critical in female suicides, 171%. Almost every English doctor has 10 to 20 possible suicide risk patients in their formal records. Dr. Norman L. Furbelow, the chief administrator of the Los Angeles Suicide Prevention Center states, "Doctors play the greatest role in suicide prevention. 50% of suicidal people will visit a doctor during the last month of their lives." At the same time, the suicide rate of British doctors is one in fifty, and in the USA approximately 100 doctors commit suicide each year.

According to statistics recorded by the World Health Organization, suicide rates in the USA are as follows:

Age 15–19	3.9 in every 100,000
Age 20–24	7.8 in every 100,000
Age 75–84	27.9 in every 100,000

This is the evident picture drawn by a civilization that is based on materialism, a civilization that does not believe in religious obligations or prohibition or in a life after death, and hence neglects the rights of its aging mothers and fathers by placing them in nursing homes.

Since they have not regarded religion and virtue as priorities of civilization, they have allowed the development of an environment which serves only the desires and temptations of the flesh. This in turn has expelled humanity out of human classification. Indeed, many have transformed into a being that has human appearance, but in terms of decorum and etiquette, they are no different than four-legged creatures that roam the earth. Making the satisfaction of their lusts and fancies the goal of their lives, they *"enjoy this world and consume (God's bounties) just as cattle consume (without considering Who has given them to them, and what they are expected to do in return, and with no sense of the life to come)"* (Muhammad 47:12). They continually quest for self-satisfaction to the extent that they deify their egoistic desires and lusts, and as such *"they are like cattle (following only their instincts)—rather, even more astray (from the right way and in need of being led)"* (Araf 7:179).

In addition, the repudiation of religious values and extreme desire for pleasures of the flesh has given birth to inequality rising from lack of compassion. Indeed, renouncement of religion has pushed the European civilization into so much chaos that it has given birth to countless sects that thrive on rebellion and defamation.

By refusing to utilize the emotions and abilities on the path prescribed by God, humanity has cast itself into chaos. As thousands of innocent people were oppressed as if they were placed into a vise, rivers and lakes were constructed from their blood and perspiration. The lack of compassion has transformed into concrete materialism. For the past few centuries, humanity has been suffering from the anguish of materialism that has frozen its delicate and sensitive emotions by attempting to remove and terminate the realm of spiritualism, the only world in which the human soul and conscience could breathe. As a result, humanity has been enslaved by a civilization that continues to crush its members, grinding them away with a system that draws the wrath of the heavens and keeps it hovering above their heads…

On the other side, we have a civilization established by the noble Prophet who stated, "By my side, the strongest amongst you is the innocent who cannot receive his rights from the tyrant; and the weakest is the tyrant who withholds the rights of the innocent." One who wants something good for himself but does not want the same thing for others has violated the basic social principles of Islam. The Prophet's principle of life was, "Support each other in altruism and religious virtue. Do not support each other in enmity and sin." According to Prophet Muhammad, peace and blessings be upon him, "A person who sleeps with a full tummy whilst his neighbor starves is not one of us." This means that if a person starves to death in the neighborhood, everyone living there will be hold accountable as murderers on the Day of Judgment.

COULD THE DAILY PRAYERS PRESCRIBED BY ISLAM BE REGARDED AS PHYSICAL EXERCISE?

We will provide some passages from an article which appeared in the March issue of Hakses Journal in 1976. The article was written by Prof. Timucin Altug who was employed by Hacettepe Hospital's emergency department at the time. These passages will offer an explanation to those who mistakenly assume that Muslim daily prayers are some form of physical exercise. There are five significant differences between prayers and regular exercise:

1. The daily prayers consist of forty *rak'ah*s, or units, in which there are eighty prostrations. Has anyone ever come across such an exercise program?

2. The prayers are performed in unhurried pace; hence they do not exert pressure on the heart.

3. The five daily prayers are performed at different times of the day. How many people who do regular sports train five times a day? What's more, the prayers cannot be abandoned in any case, during a journey or even at times of war, except if a person is insane or on his deathbed.

4. The daily prayers are an obligatory act of worship, and they have to be performed consistently until the time of death. How many people continue exercising regularly throughout their lives?

5. It is compulsory to perform ablution—the ritual of purification with water prior to a prayer. In some cases, one needs to perform complete ablution (bathing). No sportsperson goes through a ritual of ablution prior to an exercise session.

Now let us lend our ears to the doctor: The morning prayer is four *rak'ah*s; the noon prayer, ten *rak'ah*s; the afternoon prayer, eight *rak'ah*s, the evening prayer, five *rak'ah*s; and the night prayer is thirteen *rak'ah*s. So, there are forty *rak'ah*s in a day. In each *rak'ah*, or unit, of prayer, a Muslim goes to the prostration position twice. This means that a Muslim performs these movements eighty times a day. No sportsperson could follow such discipline throughout his or her life. Most sportsmen perform their exercises once a day, preferably in the morning and their programs consists of twenty to thirty different movements. Their exercises consist of high-tempo movements, their heart rates increase, and they become exhausted at the conclusion of the program. Since they do not repeat the program for the rest of the day, their bodies continue to collect calories that gradually turn to fat. Whereas, prayers are performed in slow tempo; hence the heart rate is kept under control. The movements are performed throughout the day so the performer revitalizes his or her body throughout the day. This in turn prevents the stocking of calories and the development of fat.

Blood has a vital role in human life. The heart pumps blood to the remotest parts of the human body. In order to function in the most efficient manner, the heart needs to be kept in perfect condition. In addition to this, it is imperative that we support our heart's most important function of distributing blood to our cells by keeping our body healthy through regular exercise. Just as plants need to be watered regularly, living tissues also need to be watered with blood by using the irrigation structure we call the circulatory system.

Let us explain this with an example: It is quite obvious that the amount of blood that will travel to the brain will be different if we compare a person who walks around in an upright position all day and does not perform the daily prayers to a person who goes to the prostration position eighty times a day. This also means that a person who performs the daily prayers has a blood rush to the hairy skin of his or her head eighty times a day. The meninges—the system of membranes that envelopes the brain—are fed with blood eighty times more each day for a person who performs the daily prayers in comparison to people who do not pray. This also means that the circulation in the sinuses is eighty times more for those who pray. The frontal lobe of the brain, which involves emotions and memory, is also nourished with blood eighty times more for those who pray. Cases of personality disorders and memory deficiencies are much less in those who perform the prescribed daily prayers. People who pray have a longer lifespan and do not develop dementia. The surgical procedure for dementia involves an incision to the frontal lobe of the brain. Thankfully, people who pray and go to the prostration position eighty times a day do not face the risk of such surgical procedures. In most cases, those who develop disorders such as dementia, bladder, and lower intestine problems are people who do not perform the daily prayers.

The parietal lobe in the brain integrates sensory information from different modalities, particularly determining spatial sense and navigation. This lobe also receives the benefit of being nourished with blood eighty times more in the brains of those who pray. Likewise, *the occipital lobe* that controls vision, hearing, smell, and taste also receives blood eighty times more in those who perform the daily prayers.

One does not need to be a medical scientist to realize the benefits of the additional blood rush to the cerebellum, the small brain that plays an important role in motor control. We can illuminate this with an analogy: a medicine that has been sitting in a cabinet at a pharmacy for a few years will not produce the same effect as a medicine that goes through a shaking process eighty times a day. Obviously, well-shaken medicine will mix better and will be homogeneous; therefore, it will be more effective.

Moreover, blood circulates eighty times more through the eyes of those who perform the daily prayers. This keeps the pressure in the eye under control; hence it decreases the risk of glaucoma. Glaucoma is a disorder that causes an increase in the pressure inside the eye. When the pressure is too high, damage occurs to the optic nerve. People who perform the daily prayers also benefit from the blood rush to their ears. Additional circulation of blood helps stop the formation of sinus in the frontal, ethmoid, sphenoidal, and maxillary sinusitis.

Daily prayers also increase the blood circulation in the esophagus and the teeth roots, preventing the development many diseases. Once again, the blood circulation in the ganglion cells is enhanced with the daily prayers. The apex caverns in the human lungs do not fill with blood in most cases, particularly in people with certain illnesses. Unfortunately, these regions are the most suitable locations for the appearance of tuberculosis caverns. It is quite obvious that the lungs of people who pray five times a day, filling their apex caverns with blood eighty times more than those who do not pray, will be less likely to develop tuberculosis caverns. The movements in the daily prayers also help the reabsorbing process of the fluid buildup in the pleural. The daily prayers help the functions of various other organs in our bodies. Organs situated under the diaphragm get their share of the benefits derived from the movements performed in the daily prayers. The movements help the digestive system by aiding the stomach in the mixing process; they help the flow of liquid in the gallbladder, preventing fluid buildup; they help the process of enzyme release in the pancreas, and the rhythmical moves performed during the prayers prevent the building of fat in the greater omentum, which also reduces the risk of peristalsis problems that develop in the intestines and the bowels. Complaints of constipation are quite rare in people who perform the daily prayers. We would have to add also that kidneys and kidney glands of those who pray function more efficiently. The movements performed eighty times a day during prayers prevent the collection of sediments in the kidney pelvis and the development of kidney stones through continuous shaking of the urethra. The movements also help the bladder expel urine out of the body.

People who perform the daily prayers work the joints in their knees, elbows, wrists, shoulders, and ankles like a machine that operates constantly. It is quite apparent that this prevents the development of many disorders such as rheumatism and joint degenerations. These types of disorders are very rare in Muslims who practice their religion.

DIVINE WISDOM IN REGARDS TO THE TIMES OF THE DAILY PRAYERS

Referring to the times of the daily prescribed prayers, God Almighty says in the Qur'an, "*So glorify God when you enter the evening and when you enter the morning—and (proclaim that) all praise and gratitude in the heavens and on the earth is for*

Him!—and in the afternoon and when you enter the noon time" (Rum 30:17–18).

a. Why do we perform the daily prayers at designated times?

Each of the times of prayer marks the start of an important turning-point, so also is each time a mirror to the Divine disposal of power and the time for the manifestation of the universal Divine bounties within that disposal. Thus, more glorification, praise, and exaltation of the All-Powerful One of Glory have been ordered at these defined times. Indeed, the offering of glorification, praise, and thanks to Almighty God is the heart of the prescribed prayers. That is to say, uttering *Subhan Allah* ("Glory be to God") by word and action before God's glory and sublimity is to hallow and worship Him. It is glorifying God with the Attributes belonging and fitting for Him and declaring Him to be above having any attributes that are never fit for Him such as having defects, partners, begetting, or being begotten. And proclaiming *Allahu Akbar* ("God is the All-Great") through word and act before His sheer perfection is to exalt and magnify Him. And saying *Alhamdulillah* ("All praise be to God") with the heart, tongue, and body is to offer thanks before His utter beauty. That is to say, glorification, praise, and exaltation are like the seeds of the prayers. That is why these three things are present in every part of the prayers, in all the actions and words. And it is also why these blessed words—*Subhan Allah*, *Alhamdulillah* and *Allahu Akbar*—are each repeated thirty-three times after the prayers, in order to strengthen and reiterate the prayers' meaning. The meaning of the prayers is confirmed through these concise summaries.

b. What is the meaning of worship?

The meaning of worship is this: that the servant sees his own faults, impotence, and poverty, and in the Divine Court prostrates in love and wonderment before Divine perfection, Divine mercy, and the power of the Eternally Besought One. That is to say, just as the sovereignty of Divinity demands worship and obedience, so also does the holiness of Divinity require that the servant sees his faults through seeking forgiveness, and through his glorifications and declaring *Subhan Allah* ("Glory be to God"), he proclaims that his Sustainer is pure and free of all defects, is exalted above and far from the false ideas of the people of misguidance, and is hallowed and exempt from all the faults in the universe. And the perfect power of Divinity requires that through understanding his own weakness and the impotence of other creatures, the servant proclaims *Allahu Akbar* ("God is the All-Great") in admiration and wonder before the majesty of the works of the Eternally Besought One's power, and bowing in deep humility he seeks refuge in Him and places his trust in Him. And the infinite treasury of Divinity's mercy requires that the servant makes known his own need and the needs and poverty of all creatures through the tongue of questioning and supplication and that he proclaims his Sustainer's bounties and gifts through thanks and laudation and uttering *Alhamdulillah* ("All praise be to God.") That is to say, the words and actions of the prayers comprise these meanings and have been laid down from the side of Divinity.

c. How can we explain the notion that the daily prayers consist of all forms of worship?

Just as man is an example in miniature of the book of universe and the opening chapter of Al-Fatiha a radiant sample of the revealed book of the Qur'an of Mighty Stature, so too are the prescribed prayers a comprehensive and luminous index of all varieties of worship and a sacred map pointing to all the shades of worship of all the classes of creatures.

The prayer is a luminous index that contains all types of worship. It is a map that points to the colorful worship of all living species. For example, there is fasting in the daily prayers because it is forbidden to eat or drink after the person enters into the consecrated state of the prayer. There is alms (*zakat*) in the prayer because prayers are the alms of human lifespan. There is holy pilgrimage to the House of God (*Hajj*) in the prayer because the praying person must face the direction of the Ka'ba, the House of God, in the prayer. Obviously, the *shahadah*, or testimony of faith, is included in the prayer. Moreover, some angels perform their worship in an upright position, whilst some remain in a bowing position and others in the prostration position. There are also angels that worship God in a sitting position. Some angels continuously recite, *Allahu Akbar* ("God is the All-Great"), whilst others repeat, *Alhamdulillah* ("All Praise be to God"), and even others chant, *Subhan Allah* ("Glory be to God"). In fact, angels perform only a certain part of the prayer and recite only the certain section of the recitations in a most tranquil and serene manner, receiving an utmost spiritual pleasure from their worship. Since all of the above components are present in the prayer, human beings perform all of them.

On the other hand, the worship of the prayer contains all forms of worship performed by the entire creation. Every creation is in a state of submission to God and worships Him in a manner that suits them. Heavenly bodies with their rising and setting motions repeat the movements of the prayer. Mountains stand upright just as we do in the *qiyam*, or standing position of the prayer. Four legged animals stand bowing just as we bow low with the hands on our knees in the *ruku* position. And plants stand in a prostration position just as we do in *sajdah*. We prostrate ourselves on the ground, with nose and forehead on the floor, in a posture of humility like the grass and trees which continuously drink water and minerals with their mouth-like roots from the soil. According to holy Qur'an, one of the main objectives of water is to clean: *"...He sent down water upon you from the sky, that thereby He might cleanse you (of all actual or ritual impurities, by enabling you to do the minor and major ablution)"* (Anfal 8:11). Indeed, how imperative is water for ablution (*wudu*) and major ablution (*ghusl*). Another verse informs us that, *"Thunder glorifies God with praises"* (Ra'd 13:13). This reminds us of the congregation uttering, *Allahu Akbar* ("God is the All-Great!") during the obligatory prayer. Just as Muslims who perform worship in large groups, birds also worship God in large flocks, *"Do you not see that all that is in the heavens and the earth, and the birds flying in patterned ranks with wings spread out glorify God? Each knows the way of its prayer and glorifica-*

tion. *God has full knowledge of all that they do*" (Nur 24:41). The shadow's lengthening and contraction is also a very beautiful and meaningful image of how creation prostrates in submission to its Creator:

> To God prostrate all that are in the heavens and the earth, willingly or unwillingly, as do their shadows in the mornings and the evenings. (Ra'd 13:15)

> Do they not see the things that God has created, how their shadows bend to the right and to the left, making prostration before God, and that in the humblest manner? (Nahl 16:48)

Just as the shadows of all objects shrink and stretch throughout the day in obedience to God, so do human beings by performing the standing (*qiyam*), bowing (*ruku*), and prostration (*sajdah*) positions in the prayer. In sum, this universe and all the created things and beings in it are in a state of subjugation to God and worship Him willingly or unwillingly in a manner that suits their nature. The worship of prayer is performed in the best manner when it is fulfilled spiritually and with heart. The believer prays, therefore, willingly and is rewarded for his prayers.

d. What is the Divine wisdom in the designated times of the daily prayers?

Just as the hands of a clock which count the seconds, minutes, and hours follow one another and indicate the nature and function of one another, so too do the consecutive divisions of day and night, the years, and phases of each individual's life-span in the world—which function like the hands of the huge clock of Almighty God—mirror one another. Functioning like the wheels and levers of the huge clock of Almighty God, the seconds of this immense clock correspond to the days of this world, the minutes its years, the hours its centuries, and the days its eras, and all of these resemble one another and indicate the nature and functions of one another. For example:

The time for fajr (before sunrise) may be likened to the early spring, the moment of conception in the mother's womb, and the first of the six consecutive days during which the Earth and heavens were created. It recalls how God disposes His power and acts in such times and events.

The time for zuhr (just past midday) may be likened to midsummer, the prime of youth, and the period of man's creation in the lifetime of the world, and it calls to mind God's compassion and abundant blessings in those events and times.

The time for asr (afternoon) is like autumn, old age, and the time of the Final Prophet (the Era of Bliss), and it recalls the Divine acts and favors of the All-Merciful One in them.

The time for maghrib (sunset) recalls the departure of many creatures at the end of autumn, man's death, and the destruction of the world at the commencement of the Resurrection. This time brings to mind the manifestations of Divine Glory and Sublimity and rouses man from his slumbers of heedlessness.

The time for 'isha (nightfall) calls to mind the world of darkness veiling all the objects of the daytime world with a black shroud, winter hiding the face of the dead earth with its white cerement, and even the remaining works of departed men dying and passing beneath the veil of oblivion. It reminds us of this world, the arena of examination, being shut up and closed down forever, and it proclaims the awesome and mighty disposals of the All-Glorious and Compelling Subduer.

As for *the nighttime*, through keeping in mind the winter, the grave, and the Intermediate Realm, it reminds man how needy the human spirit is for the All-Merciful One's Mercy. And the late-night *tahajjud* prayer informs him what a necessary light it is for the night of the grave and darkness of the Intermediate Realm; it warns him of this, and through recalling the infinite bounties of the True Bestower, proclaims how deserving He is of praise and thanks.

And *the next morning* calls to mind the morning following the Resurrection. Just as morning follows night and spring comes after winter, so the morning of the Resurrection follows the intermediate life of grave.

In sum, each appointed prayer time marks the start of an important turning-point and recalls other great revolutions or turning-points in the universe's life. Through the awesome daily disposals of the Eternally Besought One's power, each of the prayer times brings to mind the miracles of Divine power and gifts of Divine mercy of every year, every age, and every epoch. That is to say, the prescribed prayers, which are an innate duty, the basis of worship, and an unquestionable obligation, are most appropriate and fitting for these times.

HUMAN PSYCHOLOGY AND THE PRAYER

By nature man is extremely weak, yet everything touches him and saddens and grieves him. He is also utterly lacking in power, yet the calamities and enemies that afflict him are extremely numerous. And he is extremely wanting, yet his needs are indeed many. He is also lazy and incapable, yet life's responsibilities are most burdensome. His humanity has connected him to the rest of the universe, yet the decline and disappearance of the things he loves and with which he is familiar continually pains him. His reason shows him exalted aims and lasting fruits, yet his hand is short, his life brief, his power slight, and his patience little.

Thus, it can be clearly understood how essential it is for a spirit in this state at the time of *fajr* in the early morning to have recourse to and present a petition to the Court of an All-Powerful One of Glory, an All–Compassionate, All-Beauteous One through prayer and supplication and to seek success and help from Him. What a necessary point of support it is so that he can face the things that will happen to him in the coming day and bear the duties that will be loaded on him.

And the time of *zuhr* just past midday is the day's zenith and the start of its decline, the time when daily labors approach their achievement, the time of a short rest from the pressures of work, when the spirit needs a pause from the heedlessness and insensibility caused by toil, and a time Divine bounties are manifest. Anyone may understand then how fine and agreeable, how necessary and appropriate it is to perform the midday prayer for the human spirit, which means to be released from the pressure, shake off the heedlessness, and leave behind those meaningless and transient things, to clasp ones hands at the Court of the True Bestower of Bounties, the Eternally Self-Subsistent One, to offer praise and thanks for all His gifts, and to seek help from

Him, and then to bow in display of one's impotence before His Glory and Tremendousness, and to prostrate and proclaim one's wonder, love, and humility. He who does not understand this is not a true human being...

As for the time of *asr* in the afternoon, it calls to mind the melancholy season of autumn, the mournful state of old age, and the somber period at the end of time. It is also when the matters of the day reach their conclusion, the time the Divine bounties which have been received that day—health, well-being, and beneficial duties—have accumulated to form a great total, and the time that proclaims through the mighty sun hinting by starting to sink that man is a guest-official and that everything is transient and inconstant. The human spirit desires eternity and was created for it; it worships benevolence and is pained by separation. Thus, anyone who is truly a human being may understand what an exalted duty, what an appropriate service, what a fitting way to repay a debt of human nature, indeed, what an agreeable pleasure it is to perform the afternoon prayer, for by offering supplications at the Eternal Court of the Everlasting Pre-Eternal One, the Eternally Self-Subsistent One, one takes refuge in the grace of unending, infinite Mercy. By offering thanks and praise in the face of innumerable bounties, by humbly bowing before the Mightiness of His Divinity, and by prostrating in utter humility before the Everlastingness of His divinity, one finds true consolation and ease of spirit, girded and ready for worship in the presence of His Grandeur.

And the time of *maghrib* at sunset recalls the disappearance amid sad farewells of the delicate and lovely creatures of the worlds of summer and autumn at the start of winter. And it calls to mind the time when through his death, man will leave all those he loves in sorrowful departure and enter the grave. And it brings to mind the time of the death of this world when amid the upheavals of its death-agonies, all its inhabitants will migrate to other worlds, and the lamp of this place of examination will be extinguished. And it is a time that gives stern warning to those who worship transient, ephemeral beloveds.

Thus, at such a time, for the *maghrib* prayer, man's spirit, which by nature is a mirror desirous for an Eternal Beauty, turns its face towards the throne of mightiness of the Eternal Undying One, the Enduring Everlasting One, Who performs these mighty works and turns and transforms these huge worlds, and declaring God is the Creator of these transient beings, withdraws from them. Man clasps his hands in service of his Lord and rises in the presence of the Enduring Eternal One, and through saying, *alhamdulillah* ("All praise be to God"), he praises and extols His faultless Perfection, His peerless Beauty, His infinite Mercy. And when he declares: *You alone do we worship and from You alone we seek help,* he proclaims his worship for and seeks help from His unassisted Divinity His un-partnered Lordship, His unshared sovereignty. Then he bows, declaring together with the entire universe his weakness and impotence, his poverty, and baseness before the infinite majesty of the limitless power and utter mightiness of the Enduring Eternal One, and he says: All glory to my Mighty Sustainer, and glorifies his Sublime Sustainer. He prostrates before the undying Beauty of His Essence, His unchanging sacred attributes, His constant everlasting perfection, and through abandoning all things

other than Him, man proclaims his love and worship in wonder and self-abasement. He finds an All-Compassionate Eternal One, and saying, All glory to my Exalted Sustainer, he
declares his Most High Sustainer to be free of decline and
exalted above any fault.

Then, he testifies to God's Unity and the Prophethood of
Muhammad, peace and blessings be upon him. He sits, and
on his own account offers as a gift to the Undying All-Beauteous One, the Enduring All-Glorious One the blessed salu-
tations and benedictions of all creatures. And through greet-
ing the Most Noble Prophet, he renews his allegiance to him
and proclaims his obedience to his commands. In order to
renew and illuminate his faith, he observes the wise order in
this palace of the universe and testifies to the Unity of the
All-Glorious Maker. And he testifies to the Prophethood of
Muhammad the Arabian, peace and blessings be upon him,
who is the herald of the sovereignty of God's Divinity, the
proclaimer of those things pleasing to Him, and the inter-
preter of the signs and verses of the Book of the Universe. To
perform the *maghrib* prayer is this. Thus, how can someone
be considered to be a human being who does not understand
what a fine and pure duty the prayer at sunset is, what an
exalted and pleasurable act of service, what an agreeable and
pleasing act of worship, what a serious matter, and what an
unending conversation and permanent happiness it is in this
transient guest-house?

At the time of *'isha* at nightfall, the last traces of the day
remaining on the horizon disappear, and the world of night
encloses the universe. As the All-Powerful and Glorious One,
the Changer of Night and Day, turns the white page of day

into the black page of night through the mighty disposals of His Divinity, it brings to mind the Divine activities of that All-Wise One of Perfection, the Subduer of the Sun and the Moon, turning the green adorned page of summer into the frigid white page of winter. And with the remaining works of the departed disappearing from this world with the passing of time, it reminds us of the Divine acts of the Creator and of Life and Death in their passage to another, quite different world. It is a time that calls to mind the disposals of the Creator of the Heavens, the Earth's Awesomeness, and the manifestations of His Beauty in the utter destruction of this narrow, fleeting, and lowly world, the terrible death-agonies of its demise, and in the unfolding of the broad, eternal, and majestic World of the Hereafter. The universe's Owner, its True Disposer, its True Beloved and Object of Worship can only be the One Who with ease turns night into day, winter into spring, and this world into the Hereafter like the pages of a book which only He writes, changes, and erases.

Thus, at nightfall, man's spirit, which is infinitely impotent and weak, infinitely poor and needy, plunged into the infinite darkness of the future, and tossed around amid innumerable events, performs the *'isha* prayer, which has this meaning: Like Abraham, man says: *I do not love those that set,* and through the prayers seeks refuge at the Court of an Undying Object of Worship, an Eternal Beloved One, and in this transient and dark world, in this fleeting life and black future, he supplicates an Enduring, Everlasting One. And for a moment of unending conversation, a few seconds of immortal life, he asks to receive the favors of the All-Merciful and Compassionate One's Mercy and the light of His guidance, which will strew light on his world, illuminate his future, and bind up the wounds resulting from the departure and decline of all creatures and friends.

And temporarily man forgets the hidden world, which has forgotten him, and he pours out his woes at the Court of Mercy with his weeping, and whatever happens, before sleeping—which resembles death—he performs his last duty of worship. In order to close favorably the daily record of his actions, he rises to pray; that is to say, he rises to enter the presence of an Eternal Beloved and Worshipped One in place of all the mortal ones he loves, in the presence of an All-Powerful and Generous One in place of all the impotent creatures from which he begs, in the presence of an All-Compassionate Protector so as to be saved from the evil of the harmful beings before which he trembles.

And he starts with Surah al-Fatiha, that is, instead of praising and being obliged to defective, wanting creatures, for which they are not suited, he extols and offers praise to the Sustainer of all the worlds, Who is Absolutely Perfect and Utterly Self-Sufficient and All-Compassionate and All-Generous. Then he progresses to the address: *You alone do we worship*. That is, despite his smallness, insignificance, and aloneness, through man' connection with the Owner of the Day of Judgment, Who is the Sovereign of Pre-Eternity and Post-Eternity, he attains to a rank where he is an indulged guest in the universe and an important official. Through declaring: *You alone do we worship and from You alone do we seek help*, he presents to Him in the name of all creatures the worship and calls for assistance of the mighty congregation and huge community of the universe. Then through saying: *Guide us to the*

Straight Path, he asks to be guided to the Straight Path, which leads to eternal happiness and is the luminous way.

And now, he thinks of the mightiness of the All-Glorious One, of Whom, like the sleeping plants and animals, the hidden suns and sober stars are all like soldiers subjugated to His command, a lamp and servant in this guest-house of the world, and uttering: God is the All-Great, he bows down. Then he thinks of the great prostration of all creatures at the command of *Be! and it is*. At that moment all the varieties of creatures each year and each century—and even the Earth, and the universe—declare: God is Most Creative, and bow down in prostration. And like they are raised to life, some in part and some the same, in the spring at an awakening and life-giving trumpet blast from the Command of "Be! and it is," and rise up and are girded and ready to serve their Lord. Insignificant man, too, follows them declaring: "God is the All-Great!" in the presence of the All-Merciful One of Perfection, the All-Compassionate One of Beauty and in wonder-struck love, in eternity-tinged humility, and in dignified self-effacement, and he bows down in prostration. That is to say, he makes a sort of Ascension, and for sure you will have understood now how agreeable, fine, pleasant and elevated, how high and pleasurable, how reasonable and appropriate a duty, service, and act of worship and what a serious matter it is to perform the *'isha* (night) prayer.

PRAYERS AND MORALITY

If you compare a person's manners during the time when he does not pray to the time when he commences to pray, without question you will notice a significant improvement in his

morality. *"For prayer restrains from shameful and unjust deeds"*
(Ankabut 29:45). Concentrating on the character of different individuals for this comparison would be an incorrect
analysis. The correct interpretation would be this: a virtuous
person who does not pray will only improve his virtuous
character by commencing to pray, and without doubt, he
will reach the peak of morality through his commitment to
prayers.

Those who pray have at least four main advantages in life:
1. Cleanliness
2. Strong heart and mind
3. Discipline and efficient use of time
4. Social harmony (through community)

The great benefits of praying are countless. Even the most
obvious moral benefits such as destroying conceit, building
brotherhood, and developing a habit of performing deeds only
for the sake of God are significant enough to mention. For this
reason the worshipper wears his finest clothes during the
prayer and as an act of humility places his head on the ground
as he thinks about the mistakes made in the past. This is a display of sincerity, a breaking of arrogance and conceit before
God, in whom the worshipper believes genuinely as he goes to
the prostration position, over and over again. It is the mysterious relationship between *sajdah* (prostration position) and
arrogance that prevents the people of conceit from performing
the prayers. Placing the head down before God in their finest
clothes touches a nerve in the brains of haughty individuals.
"The prayer is burdensome, except to those who bring a lowly spirit"
(Baqara 2:45). Do they not think that all of the accessories and
bounties were bestowed upon them by Divine compassion and

that one day their oily foreheads will be decomposed into dust and earth? Moreover, the earth and its soil should not be disparaged and demeaned because there are times when human beings spill blood for them. Human life flows out of the earth, and it is God who makes this happen.

DOES IT BECOME TEDIOUS?

Some people say, "The Prayers are fine, but to perform them every day for five times is quite a burden. Since they never end, it becomes wearying." How do we reply to this?

1. Is your life eternal, I wonder? Have you any incontrovertible document showing that you will live till next year, or even till tomorrow? What causes you boredom is that you fancy you shall live forever. You complain as though you will remain in the world for pleasure eternally. If you had understood that your life is brief, and that it is departing fruitlessly, to spend one hour out of the twenty-four on a fine, agreeable, easy, and merciful act of service which is the means to the true happiness of eternal life, surely this would not cause boredom, but excite a real eagerness and agreeable pleasure.

2. Every day you eat bread and drink water. Do these acts cause you boredom? They do not because since they are needed, it is not boredom but pleasure that they give. Likewise, the five daily prayers should not cause you boredom, for they attract the sustenance, water of life, and air of your friends in the house of your body, your heart, spirit, and subtle faculties. Indeed, the sustenance and strength of a heart which is afflicted with infinite grief and sorrows and captivated by infinite pleasures and hopes may be obtained

by knocking through supplication on the door of One All-Compassionate and Munificent. And the water of life of a spirit connected with most beings, which swiftly depart from this transitory world crying out in separation, may be imbibed by turning towards the spring of Mercy and Eternal Beloved through the five daily prayers. And a conscious inner sense and luminous subtle faculty, which by its nature desires eternal life and was created for eternity and is a mirror of the Pre-Eternal and Post-Eternal One and is infinitely delicate and subtle, is surely most needy for air in the sorrowful, crushing, distressing, transient, dark, and suffocating conditions of this world and can only breathe through the window of the prayers.

3. O my impatient soul! Is it at all sensible to think today of past hardships of worship, difficulties of the prayers, and troubles of calamities and be distressed, and to imagine the future duties of worship, service of the prayers, and sorrows of disaster and display impatience? In your impatience you resemble a foolish commander, who, although the enemy's right flank joined his right flank and became fresh forces for him, he sent a significant force to the right flank and weakened the center. Then, while there were no enemy soldiers on the left flank, he sent a large force there and gave them the order to fire. The center was then devoid of all forces. The enemy understood this and attacked the center and routed it.

Yes, you resemble this, for the troubles of yesterday have today been transformed into mercy; the pain has gone while the pleasure remains. The difficulty has been turned into blessings, and the hardship into reward. In which case, you should not feel wearied by it, but you should instead make a serious effort to continue with a new eagerness and fresh enthusiasm. As for future days, they have not yet arrived, and to think of them now and feel bored and wearied is a lunacy similar to thinking today of future hunger and thirst, and starting to shout and cry out. Since the truth is this, you will think, if you are reasonable, of only today in regard to worship and say: "I am spending one hour of it on an agreeable, pleasant, and elevated act of service, the reward for which is high and whose trouble is little." Then your bitter dispiritedness will be transformed into sweet endeavor.

If you are intelligent, take as your guide the truth apparent in this example. Say in a manly fashion: "O Most Patient One!", and shoulder the three sorts of patience. If you do not squander in the wrong way the forces of patience Almighty God has given you, they should be enough for every difficulty and disaster. So hold out with those forces!

4. Is this duty of worship without result, and is its recompense little that it causes you weariness? If someone was to give you a little money or to intimidate you, he could make you work till evening, and you would work without slacking. So is it that the prescribed prayers are without result in this guest-house of the world, which are sustenance and wealth for your impotent and weak heart? Are they not sustenance and light in your grave, which will be a certain dwelling-place for you? And at the Resurrection, when you will anyway be judged, are they not a document and patent? And on the Bridge of *Sirat*, over which you are bound to pass, a light and a mount? And are their recompenses little? Someone promises you a present worth a hundred liras and makes you work

for a hundred days. You trust the man who may go back on his word and work without slacking. So if One, for Whom the breaking of a promise is impossible, promises you recompense like Paradise and a gift like eternal happiness and employs you for a very short time in a very agreeable duty, if you do not then perform that service or if you act accusingly towards His promise or slight His gift by performing it unwillingly like someone forced to work or by being bored or by working in halfhearted fashion, you will deserve a severe reprimand and awesome punishment. Have you not thought of this? Although you serve without slacking in the heaviest work in this world out of fear of imprisonment, does the fear of an eternal incarceration like Hell not fill you with enthusiasm for a most light and agreeable act of service?

5. Does your slackness in worship and deficiency in the prescribed prayers arise from the multiplicity of your worldly occupations, or because you cannot find time due to the struggle for livelihood? Were you created only for this world that you spend all your time on it? You know that in regard to your abilities you are superior to all the animals and that in regard to procuring the necessities of worldly life you cannot reach even a sparrow, so why can you not understand that your basic duty is not to labor like an animal, but to expend effort for a true, perpetual life, like a true human being? In addition, the things you call worldly occupations mostly do not concern you, and the things you meddle in officiously are trivial matters. You leave aside the essential things and pass your time in acquiring unessential information as though you were going to live for a thousand years.

If you say, "What keeps me from the prayers and worship and causes me to be slack are not unnecessary things like that, but essential matters like earning a living," my answer will be as follows: Suppose that you work for a daily wage of ten dollars and someone comes to you and says: "Come and dig here for ten minutes, and you will find a brilliant emerald worth one thousand dollars." If you reply, "No, I won't come, because one dollar will be cut from my wage and my subsistence will be less," of course you understand what a foolish pretext it would be. In just the same way, you work in this orchard for your living expenses. If you abandon the obligatory prayers, all the fruits of your effort will be restricted to only a worldly, unimportant, and unproductive livelihood.

However, if you pray during your rest periods, your spirit will become lively and your heart will experience ease. You also will discover two mines, both of which are important sources for a productive worldly livelihood and for your provisions for the Hereafter. First, through a sound intention, you will receive a share of the praises and glorifications offered by your orchard's plants and trees. Second, whatever is eaten of the garden's produce, whether by animals or man, cattle or flies, buyers or thieves, it will become like almsgiving from you. But on condition you work in the name of the True Provider and within the sphere of His leave, and if you see yourself as a distribution official giving His property to His creatures.

So see what a great loss is made by one who abandons the prescribed prayers. What significant wealth he loses, and he remains deprived of those two results and mines which afford him great eagerness in his effort and ensure a strong morale in his actions; he becomes bankrupt. Even as he grows old, he will grow weary of gardening and lose interest in it, saying, "What is it to me? I am anyway leaving this world, why should I endure this much difficulty?" He will cast himself into idleness. But the first man says: "I shall work even harder at both worship and licit endeavors in order to send even more abundant light to my grave and to procure more provisions for my life in the Hereafter."

Know that yesterday has left you, and as for tomorrow, you have nothing to prove that it will be yours. In which case, know that your true life is the present day. So throw at least one of its hours into a mosque or prayer-mat, a coffer for the Hereafter like a reserve fund set up for the true future. And know that for you and for everyone, each new day is the door to a new world. If you do not perform the prayers, your world that day will depart as dark and wretched and will testify against you in the World of Symbols. For everyone, each day has a private world out of this world, and its nature is dependent on each person's heart and actions. Like a splendid palace reflected in a mirror takes on the color of the mirror, if it is black, it appears black, and if it is red, it appears red. Also it takes on the qualities of the mirror; if the mirror is smooth, it shows the palace to be beautiful, and if it is not, it shows it to be ugly. Like it shows the most delicate things to be course, you alter the shape of your own world with your heart, mind, actions, and wishes. You may make it testify either for you or against you.

If you perform the five daily prayers, and through them you are turned towards that world's Glorious Maker, all of a sudden your world, which looks to you, is lit up. Quite simply as though the prayers are an electric lamp and your intention to perform them touches the switch, they disperse that world's darkness and show the changes and movements within the confused wretchedness of worldly chaos to be a wise and purposeful order and the meaningful writing of Divine power. They scatter one light of the light-filled verse, *"God is the Light of the Heavens and the Earth,"* over your heart, and your world on that day is illuminated through the reflection of that light. And it will cause it to testify in your favor through its luminosity.

Those who do not perform the prayers will never comprehend this unique essence of the universe. Things we observe as chaotic, in fact, declare the greatness of God in their own unique way and with absolute order. For example, if a savage entered a mosque on Friday to observe Muslims offering the Sunnah prayer, he would not detect order as everyone prays in their own pace, but, if he observed them praying the Fard prayer in congregation, he would recognize the perfect order. Another example is that initially trees stand straight as if they were in *qiyam* (the upright position during the prayer). Then, as they age and begin to decay, they bend into *ruku* (the bowing position during the prayer). Finally, they end up in the prostration position as they dissolve into the earth. Human life is the same: childhood, youth, middle age, old age, and death. The sun gives us a similar impression as it stands in *qiyam* during noon and then goes to prostration as it sets. Civilizations with their establishment, advancement, peak, and fall illustrate *qiyam*, *ruku*, and *sajdah* and hence testify to the greatness of the Eternal God by declaring, "God is the All-Great!" Even our emotions with their ups-and-downs follow the same rhythm...

Who Needs it?

Those who do not perform the daily prayers argue, "Does God need our prayers that He persistently cautions us in a stern manner and threatens us with terrible punishment such as the Hellfire?"

The Almighty God does not need your prayer, nor does He have need for anything. On the contrary, it is you who needs worship because you are spiritually ill, and prayers are the only cure and remedy for your metaphysical ailment. How logical would it be if a compassionate doctor persistently insisted that his ailing patient took certain beneficial medicines, and the patient argued, "Why are you insisting so much, do you have need for this?" It is evident that when the doctor insists that the patient take certain vitamins and antibiotics for a certain period of time and persistently reminds the patient of their significance, he is thinking of the wellbeing of the patient. Then, obviously we need to perform our prayers because they are the nourishment and sustenance of our spiritual emotions and metaphysical antibiotics for destroying viruses such as arrogance, conceit, carnal desires, and Satan. How could we file down our arrogance and ego without prostrating ourselves on the ground in a posture of humility and submission to God in *sajdah*, and how could we subdue our carnal desires without prostration?

The following parable will shed some light on the issue: A traveler on horseback comes across a man sleeping under the shade of an apple tree. A venomous snake slides into the

man's mouth. In order to prevent a panic, the traveler
decides not to tell the man what had happened. Quickly, he
wakes the man up and shoves a hand full of rotten apples
into his mouth. Then he mounts his horse and begins to
chase the man around the paddock. In fear of his life, the
man runs vigorously as he becomes quite upset with the
horseman. A short while later, the man's stomach turns
upside down, and he begins to vomit. Suddenly, the snake
comes out with his disgorge. The horseman dismounts his
horse and kills the venomous snake. Finally, the man under-
stands the confusing behavior of the horseman. This story
teaches us that human beings cannot always comprehend
the dangerous nature of their venomous arrogance and
snake-like ego. However, when the ego knows itself,
acknowledging its limitations and weaknesses, it gives up
resisting submission to its Creator and strives to rise to perfection by knowing and worshipping Him.

In regards to Qur'anic cautions and stern threats of punishment to those who refrain from worship, they are similar
to a punishment given by the king to an abased man who
violates the rights of the people in the kingdom. A person
who abandons worship and prayer is in serious contraven-
tion and violation over the rights of all creatures that were
created by the Sultan of eternity and infinity, the Almighty
God. The Qur'anic verse, *"The armies on earth and in heavens
above belong to God"* (Fath 48:4 and 7), clearly indicates that
everything in the universe serves as a soldier to God and thus
has value. *"The seven heavens and the earth, and all beings therein, declare His glory: there is not a thing but celebrates His praise;
and yet you understand not how they declare His glory!"* (Isra

17:44). This verse clearly indicates that in regards to their worship, everything has a value in the sight of God. Accordingly, those who refrain from worship will fail to realize the obedience and worship displayed by all creatures. Perhaps, they will deny it. As a result, they will think of them as inanimate, lifeless, and insignificant objects with no value and will bring them down from a high ranked position of God-worshipping beings, reflectors of Divine Names, and Divine messages to the level of purposeless matter.

Indeed, everyone views the universe through their own mirror. The Almighty has created the human being as a proportion or a tool of comparison to the universe. For every human being, He has created a private world. The color of this private world changes depending on the individual's heart and beliefs. For example, a miserable person who is in constant sorrow observes the universe as a realm of sorrow and despair. But a joyful person who feels contented will see the universe as a place of joy and merriment hence through contemplation and worship will realize that the entire existence worships and submits to God in their own unique way. On the other hand, a person who abandons worship through neglect or denial will—contrary to their real value—assume that the entire creation is purposeless and meaningless; therefore, he will violate their rights spiritually.

Moreover, those who refrain from worship also violate their own rights because they are not the true owners of their own physical being who is a servant of God. As a result, the True Owner cautions and threatens him in order to protect the rights of his soul from the violation caused by carnal desires.

Furthermore, God reveals to us in the Qur'an the main purpose of creation: *"I have not created the jinn and human-kind but to (know and) worship Me!"* (Dhariyat 51:56). So, those who refuse worship are behaving in contrast to divine wisdom and the purpose of their creation; hence they deserve punishment.

Seed and Tree

If you ask, "What are my simple prayers in comparison to the reality of a genuine prayer?" my answer will be as follows: Like the seed of a date-palm describes the full-grown tree, your prayers describe your tree. The difference is only in the summary and details; like the prayers of a great saint, the prayers of ordinary people like you or me have a share of that light—even if we are not aware of it. There is a mystery in this truth even if our consciousness does perceive it... But the unfolding and illumination differs according to the degrees of those performing them. However many stages and degrees there are from the seed of a date-palm to the mature tree, in the degrees of the prayers, the stages may be even more numerous. But in each degree, the basis of that luminous truth is present.

ESTABLISHING THE DAILY PRAYERS

"Those who believe in the Unseen, establish the prayer in confor-mity with its conditions..." (Baqara 2:3). It is obvious that there is a difference between the terms of "establishing the prayers" and "performing the prayers." The former indicates offering or leading the prayer in conformity with its condi-tions in an unfaltering manner with tranquility and modesty.

For this reason, establishing the prayers in exact conformity with the *ta'dil arkan* (conditions) of the prayers is compulsory and also, ordering good, forbidding evil, and preparing the necessary medium for the prayers are essential requirements of Islam. Parents training and preparing their children for prayers, brothers in faith advising each other, authorities clearing obstacles from the path of prayers and displaying great sensitivity towards the Friday prayers are all essentials duties of Islam.

Instead of the term "perform," the term *iqamah*, or establish, is used in the verse. This term carries various meanings such as to stand something up, straighten up, to continue steadfastly, to encourage, or to show sensitivity. For this reason, in place of the Arabic expression *yusalluna*, which means "they perform their prayers," the expression *yukimunassalat*, which means "they establish the prayers," was used. Let us analyze the meaning of this expression in detail: To stand something up, to rise, or to establish reminds us of the Prophetic tradition, "Prayer is the pillar of religion." In this hadith, religion is likened to a huge building, and prayer is the main pillar holding up the roof over the foundation of faith. Therefore, the verse indicates that the prayer is a gigantic pillar that should be erected and firmly established with the group of believers (*jama'ah*) and placed straightly so that it supports and protects the great, exalted dome of religion. The verse also points to the foundation of this building, which would be declared in the future, and to the decoration and beautification of its components. Indeed, religion is a colossal sanctified building. Materials of this great building are comprised of rules and principles established by the Almighty Himself. However, it is up to human beings to construct it accordingly and to live in it contentedly. As an expression, we could say that God is the architect of this building, the noble Prophet is the supervisor, and his people are the laborers. The foundations of this building should be laid deep in the hearts of the people, and it should overflow from their mouths. Its pillar should be straightened with personal prayers and erected by the congregation at the area of common perspective. Then the rest of its components should be constructed in unity. However, one should never forget that this building is not an inanimate matter; it is living. Those who come after should not only focus on living in this building that was constructed by the previous scholars. Just like a living building, it should be renewed, extended, and advanced. The building and pillar analogy illustrates the social life of Islam and the significance and value of prayers. Certainly, praying in congregation symbolizes the erection and establishment of this pillar. Praying steadfastly and with inner and exterior purity will cause an overflow of faith from the body and thus bring discipline and beauty into one's life. It is through prayers that the human interior and exterior could be purified and the heart and body could be supported.

THE SPIRITUAL ASPECT OF PRAYERS

Quite often, our unsatisfied desires and never-ending cravings take control over our subconscious and force us into depression and melancholy in most unaccepted times. Through prayer, we transform our most hidden desires into words, empty our hearts out, strengthen our hope, and ease our fears. Prayer brings matchless comfort to our hearts and removes tension. An individual without a prayer is like a dark cellar. It is through prayer that we feel closer to God. Without prayer, the human being becomes a creature who is in constant struggle in a world of darkness. Through prayer, we can overcome our ego because prayer does not recognize distances, boundaries, or space-time. Through prayers we connect our infinite weakness to the infinite power of the Almighty. Prayer gives wings to our spiritual power. It brightens our inner world. Through a prayer, we can challenge the universe, not by using our limited strength but by using the power of God.

During the prayer, we ask the Almighty God to show us the right path, to protect us from evil and give us strength each time we say, "*You alone do we worship and from You alone do we seek help. Guide us to the Straight Path; the Path of those whom You have favored, not of those who have incurred (Your) wrath (punishment and condemnation), nor of those who are astray.*" We thus protect our human values and set out for our journey of ascent to the proximity of our Lord. At the same time, we accumulate immense energy by connecting our infinite weakness to God's infinite power. In time, all accumulators lose power and die out. They need to be recharged. Likewise, our body loses its balance due to external pressures and effects. Prayers are the only thing that can feed our soul through divine inspiration and supply energy to our spiritual side. A person who contemplates the Might and Power of God will move into a phase of amazement and awe. In other words, he or she will feel emotions of shock, awe, bewilderment, and fear. Every prostration position contains these feelings of astonishment and perplexity. In the physical world, just a small portion of paprika adds flavor to our food; these emotions add aroma and supply inimitable pleasure to our soul. They purify the soul of all forms of filth.

It is common knowledge that when a compassionate mother reprimands her child, the child runs back into her arms. There is pleasure concealed in the fear that the child experiences at that particular moment. The reason for this is the child is embraced by the arms of compassion. In fact, the compassion of all mothers is only a twinkle of God's infinite compassion. This means there is great pleasure in the fear of God. If fear of God contains so much pleasure, imagine the amount of pleasure that love of God contains.

Feelings, emotions, and desires incarcerated and held within will grind our soul like a malicious demon. This will eventually lead to mental disorders that leave great scars in our soul. However, through prayers, these emotions and desires will ascend and thin out. As a result, these powerful feelings that accumulate in our soul and wait like a ticking bomb transform into religious contentment and enthusiasm by altering their directions and objectives. The Almighty informs us in the holy Qur'an, "Prayers will protect human beings from evil and revolting acts." In our daily lives, perhaps we have darkened our conscience through intentional or inadvertent acts. And this may have damaged our soul and ego due to feelings of regret and disappointment. The feelings of disappointment and regret impair our ego and character without realization. This is where prayers step into preventing the emergence of these evil powers that are ready to explode. It acts as a brake-system for evil and wicked deeds. Bacteria carrying a foreign object that penetrates our skin will eventually cause an infectious wound, whether we realize it in time or not. Just as the example, sins and evil deeds also cause serious wounds in our soul. In time, without even realizing it, these spiritual wounds will erupt into serious complications. It is through God and prayers that we can destroy and expel these harmful infections of the soul and purify our spiritual essence.

Today, many physical ailments are thought to be caused by psychological and spiritual problems. There are so many physical illnesses that become chronic due to bad thoughts, anxiety, and worries. Modern medicine established a branch that conducts research on physical-spiritual health. Let us take a look at some passages by Rebecca Beard, "According to researchers, grief causes severe energy loss rather than being a simple harmless anxiety. Patients suffering from severe grief should be supported with sugar through their blood so that energy levels could be raised. If the grief period is short, the body will automatically recover and balance itself out, but if the period is prolonged and grief is suppressed, the body will react by using up its sugar reserves supplied through food. Most assume that this is a normal response that the body gives, in certain moments of anxiety. However, the abnormal form of grief is the one that is kept within and saved in the subconscious. In such cases, the body works tremendously to supply sugar to the blood. As a result, the pancreas fails to keep up with the pressures originating from sad emotions. Hence, living cells fail to perform their functions accordingly. Consequently, they do not produce enough insulin to burn off the sugar in the blood stream. Therefore, the patient develops diabetes. We try to reduce the effects of diabetes by giving insulin to the patient. However, we cannot cure the illness altogether. On the other hand, human beings can protect themselves from such illnesses by calming their anxiety and fears through prayers and worship. These spiritual acts also clean out the subconscious. This is quite a difficult task because people who have diabetes usually refrain from speaking about sad and depressing problems. This problem can only be defeated through determination and prayers. Furthermore, it has been discovered that due to depression and misery, stomach cells receive more blood than the usual amount and therefore produce extra amounts of acid which is used for digesting proteins. The excess amount of acid begins to damage the inner walls of the stomach leading to illnesses such as stomach ulcers."

There are so many people whose souls are starving due to absence of worship and prayers. Unfortunately, the comforts of modern civilization, luxuries of technology, and wealth have failed to provide happiness for them. The biggest fear possessed by these unfortunate individuals who have no inner peace is being left alone with their conscience. Perhaps, their laughter and outrageous celebration may mask their inner reservations, but this cannot stop their anxieties from eating them away on the inside. One must never forget that the soul needs nourishment as much as the physical body. Ideologies and principles that neglect these realities are dragging humanity into depression and preparing a disastrous future by taking away the most important thing from human beings—inner peace.

We will never achieve happiness and contentment in both worlds unless our soul is illuminated with the light of faith, divine commandments are fulfilled, and our inner worlds are brightened with worship and prayer.

Today, scientists have discovered many viruses and bacteria that cause a variety of illnesses. Sometimes, we live with these disease causing bacteria for many years and do not fall ill; but one day, they can suddenly bring us down, and we wonder why? The main reason this happens is that in the beginning, our immune system was strong enough to overcome these viruses. Then why do our bodies lose their resistance, all of a sudden? Body and mind experts relate this to psychological reasons. Various types of psychological disorders such as depression, stress, extreme level of grief, anxiety, and lack of faith and hope affect our cells that have taken on the duty of protecting our body. The immune system becomes paralyzed; hence viruses claim victory. Then the battle is lost. Indeed, "If there is hope, there will be no defeat."

ISLAM AND CLEANLINESS

The Qur'an tells us that "*God loves those who are clean*" (Tawba 9:108), and "*...whoever purifies himself does so for the benefit of his own soul*" (Fatir 35:18). Some of the hadiths that refer to cleanliness are as follows:

"One of the rights God has over Muslims is that they perform *ghusl* (full body ablution), washing their head and body at least once a weak."

"Those who go to bed with the scent of oil or fat on their hands should only blame themselves if they catch a disease, or get attacked by bugs or pests."

"The blessing of food is in washing the hands before and after eating."

"When you wake up from sleep, wash your hands three times before placing them into a food bowl because you do not know where they have been during the night."

"Brush your teeth with a *miswak* (or toothbrush), for this practice comes from cleanliness; cleanliness leads to faith, and faith takes its practitioner to Paradise."

And God states in the holy Qur'an: *"O you who believe! When you rise up for the Prayer, wash your faces and your hands up to the elbows, and lightly rub your heads (with water), and (wash) your feet up to the ankles. If you are in a state of ceremonial impurity bathe your whole body"* (Maeda 5:6).

According to research conducted in modern labs of today, great number of bacteria and microbes dwell under our fingernails, in particular the famous *coli bacillus*. Our Prophet has drawn attention to this many centuries ago by warning people about the dangers of these infectious organisms.

MINOR AND MAJOR ABLUTIONS (*WUDU'* AND *GHUSL*)

For quite a long time, westerners did not comprehend the significance of ablution and personal hygiene, such as cutting the fingernails and toenails or shortening certain areas of facial hair. At one time in history, they were so ignorant to the reality of ablution that during the Spanish Inquisition, authorities would arrest people who performed ablution and bring them before the inquisition courts to be severely punished. However, it all changed with the discovery of microbes and bacteria. The great scientific revolution enabled people to understand the deep wisdom concealed within Islamic practices as these biological mysteries were solved one by one.

Since the emergence of our Prophet Muhammad, peace and blessings be upon him, Islam has commanded its followers to keep their bodies clean and their personal hygiene in tip-top shape. Though it took so many centuries to truly understand the mystery behind the instructions of God and His Messenger regarding cleanliness and ablution until the discovery of germs, the Prophet, peace and blessings be upon him, warned us about the fact that nails, for instance, can be a host for harmful organisms (germs). He once said to Ali ibn Abi Talib, "O Ali, cut your long nails, for harmful things live under long nails" (Daylami, *Firdaws*, 3/205). With the advancement of medical sciences and preventive medicine, everyone realized that Islamic prescriptions regarding ablution and cleanness were not based on the hot weather conditions of the Arabian Peninsula. Certainly, it became evident that these decrees belonged to an All-Wise God, whose wisdom holds *"whatever enters the earth and comes forth out of it (such as moisture, plants, and various animal life-forms, including germs), and whatever ascends to the heavens (such as vapor and supplications) and descends from it (such as rain, light, and angels)"* (Hadid 57:4).

The religion of Islam commands us to wash our hands, feet, mouth, nose, and ears. In addition to this, we are required to wash our entire body, and this becomes compulsory in some situations and a Prophetic tradition in others. It also suggests that we clean our teeth and tongue using the *miswak*—a cleaning twig made from the branches of Salvadora Persica tree with a beautiful fragrance, or a toothbrush. Our Prophet advised people to wash and comb their hair on a regular basis. He practiced this on a daily basis. Whenever he traveled, he would carry a comb and mirror with him. He stated, "Whoever has hair should honor it." Thus, he emphasized the importance of both the tidiness and cleanliness of hair.

It is a known fact that bacteria and microbes exist on almost everything on earth. We use our hands for many different tasks such as shaking hands, giving and taking, eating and drinking, preparing food, rubbing our eyes and various organs, and for wiping. For this reason health experts believe that hands are the foremost limbs that need to be cleaned thoroughly and on regular basis. They are the parts of our bodies that come into contact with harmful bacteria most frequently. Moreover, small injuries and gashes that occur in our hands are the gateways for harmful bacteria to enter our bloodstream to cause various diseases, sometimes fatal ones.

This means Islam's commands regarding washing the hands daily and on a regular basis corresponds with modern medicine. With this we also realize the significance of washing the hands which would often be used to place food into the mouth.

In regards to our mouth, this organ comprises components such as saliva glands, teeth, and tongue. The process of digestion begins in the mouth with chewing. Bacteria that exist in the mouth will be swallowed with the food and travel down to the stomach where it will cause various complications in the digestive system. In addition, leftovers also travel to our stomachs with our saliva and cause complications by increasing the number of harmful bacteria. People who complain about stomach problems are usually advised by their doctors to look after their mouth hygiene and clean their teeth regularly. Health experts caution people about mouth hygiene emphasizing the dangers of neglecting the regular cleaning of the mouth. For this reason, Islam has been adamant on mouth hygiene and suggested that mouth and teeth should be cleaned thoroughly following each meal and they should be brushed with a *miswak* or toothbrush.

Perhaps, it was because of the bacteria-destroying qualities of brushing with a *miswak* that encouraged the Prophet to make the following statement: "If I did not refrain from burdening my people, I would have ordered them to use *miswak* before each prayer." The term order should be defined as *fard*, which means an obligatory religious act.

In addition to this, washing the mouth helps clean out the food remains that get stuck on our teeth. This in turn supports the functioning of saliva glands and capillaries.

The nose is an organ that was created to detect scent and to breathe through. For this reason, microbes that travel on dust particles use the nose to enter our bodies. In order to reduce this risk, the Almighty with His infinite wisdom created tiny hairs inside our noses. These tiny hairs serve as barriers that block out harmful substances from entering our lungs and blood vessels. Microscopic examination of the nasal cavity proves this reality hence supports Islam's prescription of washing the nose. These harmful substances travel into the nose with the intake of air, and then they get stuck on the inner walls of the nasal cavity, where they are prevented from going down to our lungs. For this reason, during ablution we wash out these harmful substances with the water we pull into our nose. Our noble Prophet instructs us to wash our mouths and noses thoroughly during ablution. These important practices are repeated during both *wudu'* and *ghusl*.

The washing of our face each time we perform *wudu'* and *ghusl* is also compulsory and has many benefits. Rubbing our faces with water strengthens the skin; it gives lightness to our heads and helps the circulatory system. It also cleans out perspiration and other discharges from the skin, giving it a better chance to breathe. Washing the face also supports the functioning of our perspiration glands. Therefore, our bodies feel revitalized and rejuvenated. Modern preventative health emphasizes the importance of facial wash, especially cleaning the mouth, nose, and the eyes.

There is great Divine wisdom in wiping the head with a wet hand during ablution (*masah*). Our brains are extremely busy thinking and contemplating continuously, and this develops fatigue. The rush of blood and weariness has a significant impact on our brain; a touch of water relaxes it and allows it to function better.

The thorough cleaning of the ears plays an important role in the prevention of the influenza virus. Moreover, applying water on our arteries that carry blood to the brain helps the blood circulation system.

The main reason for washing the feet is hygiene. If the skin between the toes is not cleaned properly, it will be a breeding ground for many types of bacteria. According to medical research, diseases such as tetanus and other acute infectious diseases can easily be contracted through the skin between our feet.

For these and many other reasons, Islam has commanded ablution prior to each prayer and full body ablution (*ghusl*) when it becomes necessary. The full body ablution is also prescribed by the noble Prophet before the Friday and Eid prayers. Indeed, Islam does not command *ghusl* to be repeated on regular basis, and the reason for this is not to place too much burden on its followers. There is also a reason for excluding the parts of our bodies not washed during ablution (*wudu'*); the rest of our body is covered with clothing which serves as protection against many external dangers.

A full body ablution performed accordingly has many benefits. Medical science regards this as an important procedure. It cleanses the skin and softens it; it rejuvenates the body; it relaxes the nervous system; it relaxes the body and makes sleep easier; and it unwinds the brain and helps the function of the perspiration glands. Prophet Muhammad, peace and blessings be upon him, said to Abu Darda, "Show care to your hygiene so that you may live long." The Prophet's advice has been realized now by modern doctors and preventative medicine. They also conclude that ablution and hygiene prolongs life.

Performing ablutions prior to the prayers and being in a constant state of cleanliness is a means of great reward and spiritual blessings. Through the obligatory ablution performed prior to each prayer, even people who are not in the habit of looking after their hygiene are encouraged to maintain a healthy body.

The positive effect of water on our nervous system is common knowledge. The relaxing, soothing, and revitalizing properties of ablution are confirmed by all those who consistently perform the daily prayers. The performance of prayers in designated times and at certain intervals throughout the day forms spiritual and moral balance. It brings discipline and encourages free will. Prayers performed in congregation unite individuals in a common goal and objective. They strengthen mutual support, increase mutual love, and solidify brotherhood.

Istibra and Istinja (Washing after Toilet)

Cleaning the private parts after relieving oneself is called *istinja,* while *istibra* means taking care that the flow of urine has fully ceased before making ablution. Indeed, waiting for certain period after passing urine and washing up thoroughly are important ways of preventing possible health problems. Unless one waits for the release of urine to come to an end, urine spill on the body or garments will cause odor that resembles the smell of ammonia and may lead to infectious diseases. In order to protect our urinal path from becoming a bacterial haven, the urinal organ must be washed and cleaned carefully.

Taharah (washing and cleaning after defecation) gets rid of all types of harmful bacteria and filth. Since the human anus contains many forms of harmful bacteria, unless it is washed with water, it will lead to infectious diseases. Washing up after using the toilet is extremely important, particularly for those who suffer from hemorrhoids because bacteria can enter the blood stream and cause blood poisoning. Washing up after a bowel movement also helps prevent the invasion of certain worms, gets rid off anal itching, contracts the bowels, prevents the rush of blood to the bowels, and helps blood circulation in the reproductive organ. It also strengthens the bladder, liver, and the intestines, and it supports the digestive system and relieves constipation. After a thorough wash, the area should be dried with toilet paper. Finally, hands should be washed thoroughly, three times to prevent the development of bacteria under the fingernails.

Wudu' (Minor Ablution)

Wudu' is a form of ritual ablution that targets specific issues. Cold water used during ablution contracts the capillaries in the skin, and then they return to their normal form. This provides great relief and benefit to the human body. First of all, it quickens the blood circulation, raises the heart beat, and causes an increase in the number of red blood cells. The respiration system functions better, and the body attains strength. There is also an increase in the amount of oxygen that the body receives and the amount of carbon dioxide it releases. Washing uncovered parts of the body cleans out toxic discharges, opens the appetite, supports the digestive system, and stimulates the skin and motion nerves. This stimulation creates a significant effect on the neck, the liver, and blood vessels of the stomach. In turn, it is passed onto all organs and glands in the human body.

Proper mouth hygiene through regular rinse with water plays a vital role in protecting the respiratory system and the digestive system from diseases caught through the mouth. Similarly, washing the mouth and the nasal cavity with cold water on a regular basis plays an important role in preventing throat infections and flu-like illnesses.

Washing the face, hands, and feet is an important way of protecting the skin from infectious diseases. It is an obvious fact that most diseases enter the body via inhabiting the skin. In a similar way, parasites also find their way into the body. Without doubt, regular wash is a good and simple method of prevention because the outer layer of the skin protects the body from foreign substances unless there is a crack in the skin. Unfortunately, these cracks usually occur due to a lack of hygiene. The skin plays a vital role in the well-being of the body. It accomplishes this by discharging sweat through the thousands of perspiration glands. Sweat contains salty and fatty substances. Once the liquid side of sweat evaporates, the oily and salty substances stick to the surface of the skin and block the tiny holes that the skin uses for discharging sweat. The sweating process continues, but the accumulation of unwanted substances begins to cause complications such as poisoning. This in turn causes various stomach problems. Without question, skin and fingernail sanitation is imperative for our health.

For this reason, washing the hands and the face a number of times a day, especially prior to and after eating, sleeping, and using the toilet are important habits of protecting our health.

Ghusl (Major Ablution)

Besides religious significance and spiritual benefits, major or full body ablution has many health benefits. Full body ablution, performed in certain circumstances, is an effective tool that gets rid of slackness and droopiness caused by the tension exerted on the nervous system. Full body ablution revitalizes the body, calms the mind down, and provides physical and spiritual relaxation. Moreover, it activates the skin and the blood circulation system, opens the appetite, removes tension, and protects from cold and flu by means of rejuvenating the capillaries.

Washing the Arms Is an Effective Heart Medicine

Washing the arms is used in the general water treatment; in particular, it is used quite efficiently in the Kneipp Bath Therapy. However, society in general does not show the necessary care towards arm baths. As a matter of fact, washing the arms has great significance for our health.

- An arm bath can be performed by placing the arms in a large bowl of cold water for approximately thirty seconds. Following the wash, arms should be dried and covered. Then, a few minutes of walking with arms in motion is advisable. This small exercise is quite important. The movements in this delicate exercise form a centrifugal force during which the greatest benefit from the wash can be obtained. These movements also help balance the body temperature. One thing to remember is that the arm bath can be performed day and night and as much as it is needed.

- Such arm baths are popular especially amongst those who complain about heart problems. Many patients who have cardiac problems have thanked me for this method. Pressures on the heart, pins and needles, and discomforts can be reduced or even cured through arm baths. It is also effective for rapid heartbeat. Furthermore, it is also a known fact that heart cramps are treated with arm baths where the both arms are placed in warm water (40 degrees) and kept in the bowl for 1-2 minutes. This method provides immediate relief. Relief for respiratory problems and asthma can also be obtained through arm bath and upright position hot body bath.

- In the treatment of rheumatic and neurologic pain in the arms, and blood poisoning, herbs and arm baths provide great assistance. During the procedure arms are dipped into warm water that contains *Heublumen Absurd* flower. Then the arms are dipped into cold water, and this is repeated throughout the day. Through the method described above, I have witnessed the curing of hands that have been seriously affected by blood poisoning.

- Having cold or very warm hands is also a sign of a problem in the blood circulation system. Similarly, constant sweating in the palms can be treated and cured through arm baths.

- People who have neurological disorders and cardiac problems can perform arm baths on twice a day basis before noon and in the afternoon.

- It is also advised for healthy persons to perform arm baths.

- Arm baths have incredible effects on health, so everyone should perform them on regular basis, especially in situations of panic attack, fatigue, and over excitement. They have a unique quality of providing calm and serenity.

- After a hard day's work, those who come home should perform an arm bath before sitting for dinner (It is

Sunnah to wash the hands before eating). This will provide comfort and relaxation so that the body will be revitalized and food will provide extra enjoyment.

- Cold water arm bath has many positive effects on human psychology and neurology. The positive effect it forms on the nervous-system also affects the heart and the brain as it relaxes the body. It also has positive effect on the blood circulation system hence it is good for people who have problems with their blood pressure.

- Arm bath is an ideal heart medicine and it has no side-effects. The most important essential of this bath is that it can be performed by anyone, rich or poor, healthy or ill.

- Arm baths also have the ability to strengthen the heart and the muscles. They are like a tranquilizer that contains all types of neurological drugs.

- Besides all the benefits described above, arm baths have an important quality about them, and that is they do not cause any health problems.

An important procedure such as this should be performed and turned into a habit of every human being. Arm baths are a gem that is bestowed upon us from the divine treasury.

Foot Bath

Washing the feet with cold water is part of the ablution that is regularly used by health scientists. It can be performed in a standing or sitting position. Foot baths can be performed for 1-2 minutes in cold water; the duration may vary depending on the water temperature.

Washing the feet has significant effects such as relaxation, calmness, and the regulation of the blood circulation. A cold water foot bath is a significant method of strengthening the body's resistance. As feet become use to the cold temperatures, the body becomes more resistant to various illnesses. Foot baths also play an important treatment role in problems such as flat foot disorder, ankle injuries, fungal infections, and varicose veins. Those who have cold-feet problem should also perform foot bath on regular basis. This can be done by placing both feet in 40 degree Celsius warm water for two minutes, followed by a minute in cold water. This method is more beneficial than a normal foot bath. It has tremendous effects on the circulatory system. For a rejuvenating effect on the skin, it is beneficial to add some herbal medicine to the first part of the foot bath (warm water part). These herbal additions maybe pine needles, Heublumen flowers, or daisies.

Kneipp treatment suggests sawdust and salt. Those who have ongoing cold-feet problems should refrain from using cold water; instead, they should begin with a short warm up exercise and then perform a warm water foot bath.

The simple foot bath we mentioned in the beginning of our paragraph should be performed by everyone each night before going to bed. This is such a beneficial and relaxing practice that people who make a habit out of this will never give it up. Those who work hard throughout the day and have blood rushing to their heads must make the daily foot bath a tradition for themselves.

Everything mentioned in Dr. Albert Schaller's book entitled *Die Kneippkur*, which was written with years of experience in cure centers, is practiced by those who regularly perform *wudu'* (ablution) in their daily lives.

This means that the religion of Islam, just as in the *wudu'* example, has provided for the well-being of human beings in regards to health, psychology, and fitness even in obligatory religious practices and worship.

Today in many advanced nations, people tend to show great interest for healthy living, so Islam's principles that display great importance to health and well-being will draw their attention. These are a few windows that lead to the great palace of Islam that has millions of windows...and a few of the thousands of doors that open into it.

Islam is not the religion of certain nation or race; it embraces the whole of humanity and invites them to eternal happiness. Those who decide to follow it will always be guided to everlasting contentment...The amazing person who conveys this religion (Prophet Muhammad, upon whom be peace and blessings) does not only represent the Arab, Turk, or the Persian. He is the guide and crown of entire humanity and the jinn. We hope that the entire humanity acknowledges and accepts him!

Kirlian Photography and Ghusl

Kirlian photography involves the photographing of the body in the presence of a high-frequency electrical field. These pictures do not capture the soul but reveal a reflection of the subtle ethereal body (or the astral double) which surrounds all living beings. Psychiatrists and biologists believe that there is a connection between this subtle biofield surrounding the human body and the indications of the health and emotional changes in the body. This means a person's fatigue or health problems can be detected through Kirlian photography. Pictures taken with the Kirlian method clearly show the difference between a healthy cell and a cancerous one. The same method also shows the condition when *ghusl* (full body ablution) is necessary with a change in color and hardening of the corona. This interesting transformation disappears once a person takes full body ablution just as the one prescribed by Islam.

Miswak and Teeth

Teeth with their solid structures can continue to survive for a long period of time even after the death of their possessor. Unfortunately, due to bad management they are the first organs to be debilitated in the human body. They are the vital tools of proper speech; therefore, losing or damaging them can also cause psychological disorders.

The front teeth and the K9s help us chop and cut the food. Losing some of these teeth will cause aesthetic problems for the face. The molars play an important role in preparing the food for digestion. Their absence can cause problems for the digestive system and deformity on the cheeks of the human face. Moreover, all of our teeth help us derive a taste from our food. The amount of pleasure received from food, which is not chewed, is quite minimal.

The biggest nemesis of teeth is the bacteria produced from the tiny pieces of food left on our teeth. These bacteria cause a yeasting affect on the food to produce acid which in turn penetrates through the tooth reaching all the way to its root. The common dental problem we call "tooth decay" occurs when bacteria enters the tooth through the cracks in the enamel. In such situations, it is imperative that a filling be done to prevent the further development of this pathological problem. This is an easy and painless method of prevention.

Preventing the development of tartar is also important for mouth and tooth health. The development of yellow stains in unhygienic teeth is quite common. If neglected for a long time, it will cause bad breath and a bitter taste in the mouth. Well-managed teeth can develop an extra thickness of about one millimeter within 24 to 48 hours. The building of unwanted stains does not only pose a threat to the enamel, but it is also dangerous for the gums. With the aid of salvia, stains cause the development of tartar.

Tartar commonly develops between the teeth and gums, showing the important connection between the two. This transforms the region into a haven for the bacteria. It causes many complications such as infections, bleeding, and eventually the death of the tooth.

A tooth twig called *miswak*, obtained from the branches and the root of the *Salvadora Persica*, was prescribed by our noble Prophet, peace and blessings be upon him. A type of tooth brush is obtained by shaving the bark (1–2 cm) off and placing the stick in water. These plants can be found in abundance from East Africa to India. It is quite economical and practical to use. Using a *miswak* is also very efficient since it is easy to carry and it helps develop a habit for regular cleaning of teeth. The fruits of this tree are edible, and the benefits of using its tooth stick can be summarized as:

1. It has antiseptic qualities.
2. Its scent activates the saliva glands hence prevents the development of bad breath.
3. Its PH composition is same as the PH composition of saliva, so unlike regular tooth brushes, it does not cause a foreign object reaction in the mouth.
4. In a research conducted at Ege University, it was found that its fibers contained anisotropic crystals which were later identified as Calcium Oxalate. This substance plays an important role in the mechanics of cleaning.
5. The same research mentioned the discovery of good bacteria called Saprophyte gram (-).
6. This botanical tooth brush can be trimmed down on weekly basis to be reused.
7. Its roots can be ground into a powder and used as a paste. The roots can be boiled to make herbal tea, effective in the treatment gonorrhea. It is also good for abdominal pain.
8. Its multifaceted use such as the size can be arranged to match the user; its fibers function the same as dental floss; and the motion of the fibers producing the same effect as an electric tooth brush makes it an inimitable tooth cleaner.

You may wish to compare the benefits of *miswak* to regular tooth brush.

MATERIALISTIC GAIN SHOULD NOT BE INVOKED INTO WORSHIP

Sincerity is the soul of worship. Sincerity means performing the prayers only because God commands it. If personal gain or benefit is invoked into worship, that prayer becomes invalid. Personal gains and wisdom can only be means for preferences, they cannot be objectives. For example, if a man performs the daily prayers because he realizes that they serve as significant exercise and his health benefits greatly, instead of performing them because God has ordered it or because it is a responsibility that will be questioned on the Day of Judgment, his prayer will not be accepted. The only benefit he will receive out of his prayers is a healthy exercise.

Logic and rationality prove this. For example, if you sent your servant to a certain location and when he returned he argued that he had fulfilled the duty not because you ordered it but because he needed to go out for a walk, would you assume that he has done his duty? Would you even continue to employ him as a servant? Indeed, sincerity is usually considered the foundation of all relations, not only with servants or workers but also with relatives, friends, and others close by.

Because of this and similar valid reasons, the religion of Islam gives great importance to sincerity or honesty of intention. If a person is going to perform a duty and if this duty is a religious obligation, then it must be done with the intention of pleasing God. It is through such assessment that we can comprehend whether we have performed our duty purely for the sake of God or for various other personal reasons. We cannot assume that we have fulfilled a religious obligation for the sake of God if we were seeking to satisfy our personal interest through worship. Moreover, if personal objectives such as protecting oneself from Hellfire and making an effort to earn Paradise were not prescribed as being part of religious obligations, they would have also been invalid objectives for worship. The requirement for worship would have been solely to please God. With this in mind, highly regarded scholars have argued that even objectives in relation to eternal life used as motivation for worship will be classified on various levels.

Distinguishing worship from tradition helps measure and separate worldly objectives from the eternal ones. Prayers performed purely for God's sake and those performed in order to attain divine pleasure and rewards in both worlds can be considered as worship. On the other hand, prayers performed for worldly objectives and benefits are nothing but habitual customs.

Encouraging human beings to look for a benefit in everything they do, including religious obligations, will teach them to be self-centered and egotistical. On the other hand, religion aims to transform these emotions that were embedded in man's natural disposition in order to teach him to be self-sacrificing and to elevate his rank.

It is, therefore, rational to think that religious obligations should not be performed for worldly objectives. God Almighty says in the Qur'an:

> Whoever desires (and strives to gain) the harvest of the Hereafter, We increase him in his harvest; and whoever desires the harvest of the world, We grant him out of that, and he has no portion in the Hereafter. (Shura 42:20)

> Whoever wishes for only the immediate gains (of this transitory life), We readily grant thereof as much as We please to whomever We will. Thereafter We consign him to Hell, wherein he will roast, disgraced and dis-

owned. But whoever wishes for the Hereafter and strives for it as it should be striven for, being a believer, then for those (who do so) their striving shall be recognized with thanks and reward. (Isra 17:18–19)

Whoever desires the present, worldly life and its outward shows, We recompense them for all that they do therein, and they are not deprived of their just due therein. It is they for whom there is nothing in the Hereafter but the Fire. All that they produced in it (this world) has come to nothing and all that they were doing is fruitless, vain. (Hud 11:15–16)

According to one hadith: On the Day of Judgment, a public crier will announce: "Whoever performed a duty for someone other than God, should go and ask for his reward from him." In another hadith, the noble Prophet states: "God shall grant the world to those who have intentions for the Hereafter but He will not grant the Hereafter to those who have intentions for the world." Indeed, the very first hadith recorded in *Sahih al-Bukhari*, "(The reward of) deeds depends on the intentions" is a good example of this. The principle expressed in the hadith is that one is rewarded for his deeds according to his real intentions and not according to his actual deeds which might be good in themselves but were motivated by an ill intention.

In addition to this, searching, discovering, and distributing the worldly benefits of religious obligations is an Islamic duty that rests upon the shoulders of every Muslim. However, this research should be done for non-Muslims who have doubts about Islamic practices, rather than for Muslims who should already have total faith in the practical side of Islam.

Obviously, Muslims should also be aware of the beautiful worldly benefits that come from religious obligations. However, this should be limited to knowledge only because fulfilling religious obligations with an intention to benefit from worldly bounties would render the worship invalid. Therefore, no matter how much benefit is obtained from worship, it should only be performed with the intention of pleasing God and earning eternal life in the Hereafter. Finally, worldly benefits and rewards may only be appreciated as secondary objectives.

MOVEMENTS PERFORMED DURING THE DAILY PRAYERS

Regular exercise plays an important role in preventative health. This is quite evident in the daily prayers. The main reason for this is the prayer times are the most advised times for exercise.

The fresh air inhaled before dawn; the break taken from work during noon; the rest period needed in the afternoon (we are aware of the impact of stresses caused by wearying incessant work); evening time when people begin to prepare for rest; and night time when we make the attempt to rejuvenate our tired bodies are the best times for exercise.

Ruku (bowing) and *sajdah* (prostration) are the most excellent movements for rejuvenating our organs through blood circulation. For this reason, the daily prayers are the biggest friend of the digestive system and appetite.

Ruku (bowing) strengthens the back muscles and helps the dissolving process of stomach fat. *Sajdah* (prostration), on the other hand, strengthens the thigh muscles and other leg tendons; it supports the digestive system and helps the blood circulation system.

Prostration also prevents the development of stomach infection that originates from weak ligaments and active glands. During a prayer, arms, legs and the head are in motion and these movements are highly beneficial to our ligaments and bones. The movements performed during the prayers help reduce the joint pain felt on knees.

The daily prayers also help the blood flow down from the top section of our body, and this has a significant impact on our blood pressure. People who suffer from high blood pressure will feel the great benefits of the prayers as soon as they begin to perform them regularly.

The daily prayers bring relief to the neurological system, regulate the heart beat, control the blood circulation, and reduce depression. It is a great treatment for those who suffer from insomnia due to depression and stress. Indeed, prayers are effective regulators of sleep. They provide relaxation, serenity, tranquility, and calm for the nerves and mind.

There are disorders that many medical experts cannot cure, but they are easily treated through the daily prayers. Prayers are like the element radium; they are the source of highly luminous light.

The positive effects of the daily prayers have also been seen in the treatment of certain pathologic conditions such as chronic tuberculosis, bone infections, infectious wounds, and many other medical conditions.

Loose-Fitting Clothes

Islam prescribes the wearing of loose-fitting clothes within and outside of the prayers. Today, many detrimental effects of wearing tight clothing have been discovered. In an article published in *Gunaydin* on August 5, 1983, Dr. Cevat Babu-na states, "health complaints in connection to wearing tight pants have increased during summer." Prof. Cavit Ozsoy states, "It is a proven fact that wearing tight pants leads to health complications." Doctors believe that wearing tight pants is unhealthy for both men and women. In particular, tight jeans worn during summer cause various health problems. It is advised that women wear loose clothing during summer to enable air circulation.

The detrimental effects of wearing tight pants:

For women:

a. The pressure applied on the lower stomach causes the uterus to sag and increases the risk of losing a baby.

b. The tight pants, especially the low-cut ones sitting low on the waist, causes abdominal pain and puts pressure on the thigh nerves, causing burns and pain on the lateral aspect of the thigh.

c. It causes urinal complications.

d. It prevents the ventilation of the reproductive organ and causes many complications such as rash, itchiness, and burns.

For men:

a. It effects the functioning of the stomach which leads to indigestion.

b. It causes problems for blood circulation.

c. It lowers the number of sperm and slows down their swim-rate. As a result, it minimizes the possibility of having children.

Should we work in a standing or sitting position?

French professor Pierre Moulin says, "Standing all day during work will affect the blood circulation and cause a disorder called varicose vein. You will feel less tired if you work in a sitting position. However, sitting for long periods of time will also cause complications in the blood circulation and in the digestive system. The most ideal system of working is standing or sitting whenever required. If the job is suitable for such method then the worker should follow this routine. What if the conditions of the workplace do not allow this? We must then keep in mind that working at a sitting position is also very harmful to our hearts."

If we analyze the daily prayers, even from this perspective, we will realize their significance on human life...

Prayers at the North and South Poles

Some questions are produced with sinister intentions. One of these questions is how do we perform our prayers at the poles. The religion of Islam does not leave any issue to dispute. It has also provided a solution for this.

According to *Sahih al-Bukhari* and *Musnad* of Ahmad ibn Hanbal, the noble Messenger of God made it clear how to determine the times of prayer in places where the days and nights are unusually long or short in a hadith in which he discussed the appearance of Dajjal with his Companions: The noble Prophet said, "Dajjal will emerge from the east and travel the earth in forty days. Some of his days are like a year compared to yours. Some are like a month, some are like a week, and some are the same as your days." The Companions asked, "Will a day's prayer be enough for the day that lasts a year?" The noble Prophet replied, "No…you will have to calculate and reorganize your prayers." (This means that a day will be as long as a year close to the two poles where the sun does not rise or set for months. However, people living in such places will not follow the movement of the Sun but the movement of the clock for their five daily prayers. So, they will not pray just five times in a year just because they have one day in the whole year. Instead, they would have to divide the days into twenty-four hours and perform the prayers accordingly).

According to this hadith, people who travel to these regions should use the prayer calendar of the nearest region and divide the days into twenty-four hours. Indeed, in such regions we do not neglect our eating, working, sleeping and bathing habits, so we should not neglect our worship such as the daily prayers and the obligatory fast of Ramadan.

THE PSYCHOLOGY OF SIN

When a sin is committed, it enters the heart and begins to darken it until such a time that it expels the light of faith out of the heart. Within every sin there is a path that leads to *kufr* (denial). If the sin is not terminated with repentance, it will transform into a tiny spiritual snake which will continue to gnaw on the heart.

In regards to the issue, it is stated in Surah Mutaffifin, "*Vow to those who are in denial…They deny the Day of Judgment. Though, every transgressing sinner denies this day. When our verses are recited to them, they say, 'These are fairy-tales of the past'. Indeed, it is not the way they assume. Verily, their sins have engulfed their hearts!*" (83:10–14) As derived from the above verses, those who deny religion and transgress are the sinners. They deny Resurrection and the Day of Judgment because this reality does not please them. They look upon God's verses as fairy-tales and myths of the past. The main thing that brings them to such conclusion is the accumulation of sins that has formed a layer of rust on their hearts. They continue to believe that their sins bring some type of profit or benefit to them. Those hearts are like rusty mirrors that have collected so much filth that they can no longer reflect or capture the good. Ahmad ibn Hanbal and Tirmidhi relate the following hadith transmitted by Abu Hurayra: "When a servant of God commits a sin, a black stain appears on his heart. If he repents and displays remorse, the stain will be removed and his heart will shine again. If he continues, the stain will spread all over, until it overwhelms his heart."

As the heart darkens with time, it begins to develop feelings of denial. For example, a man who commits a shameful act does not wish anyone to know about it, so the existence of angels and spiritual beings begin to trouble him. Even the tiniest of signs develops a yearning for denial. Similarly, a man who commits a sin that necessitates punishment in Hellfire deeply wishes that Hell did not exist, so even the smallest of sins encourages him to deny the existence of Hellfire. Also, a man who does not perform the daily prayers and refrains from his servanthood duties feels the pressures of the Almighty God's perseverance. Since he feels uneasy even from the scolding of his boss at work, God's caution gives him anxiety and tension. As a result he says, "I wish the compulsory duties of servanthood did not exist." These types of thoughts and emotions lead to the development of antagonistic feelings against God. If a tiny doubt in regards to the existence of God comes to his mind, he will grab onto it as firmly as possible as if it were solid evidence. Consequently, this will open a door to eternal destruction. Unfortunately, this poor fellow does not realize that by abstaining from the duty of servanthood that has very little burden upon him, he poses himself as a target to pain and suffering that is millions of times more intense than the burden of servanthood. He flees from a mosquito bite to accept being bitten by a snake.

RECITING QUR'AN IN THE MORNING

Reciting the holy Qur'an early in the morning with a soft tone of voice and prior to breakfast has great benefits for the health of the body and mind. The vibrations that occur within the head during recitation serve as a delicate massage on the brain. This enables the capillaries to feed the surrounding nerve cells more efficiently. Reciting the holy Qur'an with a soft tone of voice and tessitura strengthens and trains the larynx as it serves as an exercise for the throat. Those who continue to recite the Qur'an on a regular basis will keep their original voice even at an old age. The soothing effect of the recitation also helps to improve the functioning of the hipofiza situated near the brain. Since the functioning of other glands depends on this region, it also supports the efficient functioning of the general discharge system. It furthermore removes pessimism and rejuvenates the mind.

Since both the Qur'an and human beings were created by the same Supreme Being, the Qur'an contains many mysteries and codes within its harmonious letters that address the sensitive nature of man. Without doubt, the holy Qur'an is an everlasting treasure that nourishes both the mind and the heart and satisfies human's natural disposition both physically and spiritually.

CHAPTER II

The Obligatory Fast

DOES OVEREATING REDUCE THE HUMAN LIFESPAN?

The duration of the human lifespan depends on the will of God. One cannot change divine destiny. However, destiny depends on cause and effect. This means that fate is the result of both causes and effects. In any case, it is the will of God that makes the final decision, and causes cannot affect or change His will.

However, the Almighty has placed certain laws and principles on this earth, which is the realm of testing, and these causes act as a veil for His Name that manifests as *al-Hakim*, or the All-Wise. All veils will be removed on the Day of Judgment although all the apparent causes are merely a veil that covers the hand of Divine Power in this world. Therefore, everything in the universe is in absolute obedience to God, bound by the laws of the creation and operation of the universe (which we wrongly call the "laws of nature"). For this reason, the following verses state: *"No change will you find in God's way (of dealing); no turning off will you find in God's way (of dealing)"* (Fatir 35:43). *"(Such was) the way of God with those who passed before. You will never find any change in God's way*" (Ahzab 33:62). Even the miracles which are usually impossible to accomplish but performed by Prophets by the will of God indicate clearly that they are proofs of their Prophethood and that they are evidence that God is the Creator of causes.

As we analyze the apparent early deaths caused by cigarettes and overeating, which we dub as the nails in a coffin, we are tackling the issue from the perspective of natural laws and causes which were created by God. Even the beloved Prophet of God, Muhammad (peace and blessings be upon him) had to abide by natural laws as he wore double armor in certain battles and ordered the digging of a trench during the battle of Trench. We should be extremely careful in distinguishing faith from natural causes. Otherwise, one who thinks of faith as an entity that exists within natural causes will become a *Mu'tazila* (a mere rationalist in his approach to existence); and one who thinks of natural causes as properties that exist with faith will become a *Jabriya* (pre-determinist who denies the freedom of the will and makes no distinction between man and inanimate nature, inasmuch as his actions are subordinate to the *jabr*, or compulsion, of God). The Ahl as-Sunnah wa'l-Jama'ah (people representing the great majority of Muslims who are believed to be on the right path), on the other hand, analyzes and evaluates everything within its own concept.

So let us tackle the issue from apparent causes, which are the manifestations of the Divine Name *al-Hakim*, or the All-Wise:

Converting food and other substances into required energy and into living tissue is not a simple process. As soon as a morsel of food enters the mouth, all digestion sensors are activated. With the support of the central nervous system and the nerves that function to aid the digestion of food, related muscles and discharge glands go into action.

Once the necessary digestion process is completed in the mouth, the mashed up food is then sent to the stomach via a determined nerve reflex. The second phase of digestion is completed by the stomach that breaks down and absorbs the food with reflex muscle movements and churns it into a liquid. Following the third phase of digestion completed by the small intestines, the food is ready to be absorbed. The liver also begins to perform more than 450 of its various functions. The heart then takes on a duty several times more than its usual functioning rate. All of the small and large organs of the body, including its cells take part in this strenuous process.

It is because of this exhausting process of digestion that the heart and other organs of the body become fatigued, and the necessary amount of blood is not sent to the central nerve cells of the brain. It is obvious that overeating exerts an incredible amount of pressure on the body and its organs.

This is the main reason why people who eat too much and thus fail to follow a healthy diet do not live long. Every organ possesses a capacity to last for a certain time. When overworked, they lose their functionality and age rapidly.

For this reason, people who eat less, live long. It is as if their youth continues throughout their lives. This is why fasting is extremely beneficial to our health. Moreover, fasting strengthens the body's immune system and protects it from illnesses.

Modern medicine and preventative health use fasting as a means of protection against certain illnesses. Some stubborn illnesses are fought with fasting. Indeed, the great benefits of fasting and healthy diet are quite evident. These days, we witness that all doctors support their prescriptions with a list of recommended and prohibited foods. Modern medicine has realized the connection between illnesses and unhealthy diet. Muslims are well aware of the following advice: "The stomach is the home of illnesses, and a proper diet is the best medicine." The Islamic principle: "observe the fast and remain strong" is interpreted by modern science as, "Fast and remain healthy."

This is exactly what we mean when we say, "Fasting prolongs life." Certainly, the duration of life is in the hands of God. Even the healthiest person could die within a matter of hours. Modern science cannot alter the will of God. However, divine will is aware of all causes and reasons; hence, as it decides, it also takes these issues into account.

a. Fasting and Healthy Diet

Foods containing albumin produce acids and vegetables produce various bases. In turn, these substances synthesize to produce various salts. There are many different salts in our cells and tissues. If there is insufficient base in our diet, acids will not be converted to salts, and this is the first sign of poisoning. Although the body has certain reserves to balance this out, if the condition reoccurs, it will lead to health problems. Fifty percent of illnesses are caused by stomach disorders. Even though the balance of acids, bases, and salts is quite imperative, we do not eat to control this balance.

On the contrary, our eating habits depend on our taste or budget. The body needs an annual resting period, at least for a month, in order to protect itself from this unbalanced diet. The prescribed Islamic fasting breaks up the harmful fats that surround our inner organs. Fasting is similar to the process of pruning trees in which the human metabolism goes through a revitalization process. Through fasting, the body's resistance increases against certain illnesses such as diabetes, kidney and liver disorders, and cardiac and artery problems, as long as there is no overeating during the pre-dawn meal of *sahur* and the fast breaking meal of *iftar*. Alexis Carrel states, "Refraining from food develops the feeling of starvation which sometimes leads to nervous tension which eventually transforms into a feeling of weakness. However, it opens a path to some significant occurrences. Sugars in the liver, fat under the skin, and proteins in muscle and gland cells become active. All external organs begin to sacrifice valuable substances for the well-being of the heart and vital organs. Thus fasting cleans and renews our tissues."

The adaptation function of adjusting to starvation has played a great role in the continuation of the human race, and fasting regulates this by strengthening the body's resistance to hunger and dehydration.

The supererogatory fasting observed on Mondays and Thursdays regulates the hormonal function and protects those who do not release their energy through work and sports—in particular the youth—from misbehavior and misconduct. This fasting that is observed for the sake of God minimizes the bodily pressure exerted on the soul and emancipates the soul from captivity.

b. Fasting and Muscle Function

The human body moves through the functioning of muscles that are controlled by the motor nervous system which is connected to the central nervous system. In order to achieve motion, some muscles contract and some slacken. The contraction and loosening of muscles also has an impact on other organs which become enervated by the process. In order to support the functioning of the muscles, the heart and the blood circulation system use up the nourishment and nutrition that has been obtained through digestion. The more blood our muscles receive, the more functional and enduring they become. In cases of weak blood circulation, muscles become indolent and lose their vivacity.

The amount of blood delivered to our muscles depends on external conditions. Since the volume of blood in our arteries remains the same, we wonder why the amount of blood received by our muscles varies.

Our bodies are not made up of muscles only. There are many other organs that also need blood. If the required amount of blood decreases in one organ, other parts of the body benefits from this by receiving more blood.

The digestive system needs large amounts of blood in order to perform all of its duties. During the digestion of food, blood is needed for processes such as motion, discharge, conversion, and absorption. For this reason, the blood circulation system becomes quite busy throughout the digestion process, during which muscles and other organs receive less blood.

This situation weakens the body and decreases its resistance to weariness. Therefore, the body becomes indolent as it is overwhelmed by lethargy.

These days a common advice given to athletes is, "Do not eat prior to training or hard work out."

One of the hardest physical activities on earth is participating in a combat with swords. Our noble Prophet advised those who prepared for battle, "Observe the fast on this holy day."

Some weak bodies cannot endure fasting. Fasting may weaken their muscles and reduce their ability to think. Although the number of such people is not great, Islam makes considerations for their condition so that during a battle, the noble Prophet said: "Those who cannot endure the fast should break it."

Through fasting the body gains muscle strength and becomes more resistant. The endurance and abilities of muscles increase during the fast. Although the mind and body work harder during the month of Ramadan, the body does not weaken. The reason for this is that fasting provides the body an opportunity to benefit from food more efficiently. It forms a new dietary principle for the body. A person who works throughout the day with a light body regains energy through food and rest during the night.

Within the 24 hours of daily life, two designated times of food intake (*sahur and iftar*) is sufficient. Weight loss observed in some people during the fast does not occur due to lack of food. It is usually caused by lack of sleep and rest. On some occasions fasting may cause a weight increase because fasting initiates a more lively digestion. During the fast, the digestion system works better; this in turn develops a healthier appetite.

Fasting also encourages one to work more efficiently and teaches time management. In fact, eating only twice a day is the most appropriate diet. This also allows for a long period of work time. In contrast, lunch has negative effects on the human body. It weakens the system and brings indolence. The lethargic body inclines towards sleep and away from work.

When the stomach is empty, the body feels light and thus functions efficiently. During the fasting period, the two prayers (noon and afternoon) performed during the resting periods of the day provide revitalization for the body and its muscles. In addition, the prayers allow the mind to rest and enter into deep contemplation.

We do not come across a system that disciplines life's every moment with daily programs in the way it is established by Islam.

The diet method we have described above (two meals a day) is the very program that the noble Prophet Muhammad, peace and blessings be upon him, followed throughout his life.

c. Fasting and Human Health

Exercise alone is not enough to attain a healthy body. In order to keep healthy, it is imperative to follow a diet based on certain principles. Physical indolence and lassitude will entail mental and spiritual lethargy and weariness. This in turn will lead to many health problems and complications. The various illnesses we face after a certain age are the results and detrimental manifestations of previous habits.

i. Overeating and obesity

Regardless of the cause, science considers overeating as a type of medical disorder. Generally, obesity may not cause many problems until the age of forty. However, after this age, disorders such as fatigue, respiratory problems, and joint pains will begin to emerge. Illnesses such as diabetes, artery rigidity, coronary disorders, goiter, joint disorders, gall bladder stones, and heart problems are observed more frequently in obese individuals.

According to statistics, slim people live longer than those who are overweight. Problems with menstrual cycles and the ability to bear children are more common in obese women. In obese men, sperm disorders and impotence are quite common. Obesity also leads to hypoventilation disorder. The motions of the diaphragm and chest become limited by the extreme fat triggering respiratory problems. As a result, the body receives less oxygen and the function of the heart becomes insufficient. This disorder is called the Pickwickian Syndrome (also known as obesity hypoventilation syndrome).

Since obesity causes so many health complications, people should refer to disciplinary diets and fasting to preserve their health. It is a well known fact that stomach is the dwelling place of ailments, and fasting is the commencement of treatment.

Today, modern medicine considers fasting as an efficient way of treatment for various illnesses. For instance, Dr. Henri Lahman's clinic in Dresden, Saxony is renowned for treatments through fasting. The clinics of Dr. Berserbern and Dr. Molier also use this method. The core fundamentals of the treatment are to remove unnecessary food deposits from the body so that the digestive system can function more efficiently. Significant results have been obtained through this method, which lowers cholesterol levels to enhance the blood circulation system and salt levels to control high blood pressure. In addition, urinal disorders and neurological problems are also treated through diet.

In the past, the health benefits of eating less were general public knowledge as well. People knew a lot about how fasting and diet could help them enhance and restore their health. Historically, for instance, there is evidence of a connection between healthy living and eating less during the time of Suleyman the Magnificent. It is a well-known fact that Prophet Muhammad, peace and blessings be upon him, always contented himself with eating less, and it is evident in the traditions that he used to leave the dining table without fully satisfying his hunger. Indeed, he advised eating less by dividing the stomach into three parts: one third for food, one third for drink and the other for breath.

In addition to these common diseases mentioned above, other illnesses begin to emerge due to excessive food intake and consumption of alcohol. Some of these illnesses are: Mallery Weis Syndrome, Pancreatic infection, and Zieve's Syndrome (a liver disorder).

Endocrinology experts claim that people who overeat are more likely to develop diabetes. Cardiologists have discovered a link between heart attacks and overeating.

As all of the above suggests, fasting and disciplinary diet are essential for human health.

Prof. C. L. Paul Trieb of the Cancer Institute in Nordheim Westfalen, Germany has discovered that fasting protects people from developing cancer. According to a popular paper by Prof. Trieb, large amounts of adrenaline and cortisone hormones mix into the blood in the bodies of those who fast. These hormones that control the numbers of cells in the human body also have implacable effect on cancer cells. They block the development of cancerous cells.

Prof. Kazim Gurkan states: "Fasting is a type of disciplinary diet. We have to remember that during the era when fasting was prescribed as a best method of treatment, people had no knowledge about cholesterol, high blood pressure, and lipids. For this reason, I have great respect for this religious diet; by this I mean fasting."

ii. Why does fasting coincide with different seasons?

Based on the lunar year, the Islamic calendar is eleven days shorter than the solar year; therefore, it moves and retrogresses each year in relation to the solar calendar and completes the cycle every 32 years. For this reason, the month of Ramadan falls in various seasons and constantly changes from year to year. Thus, it does not pose a constant challenge for the believers who have to observe their fast in the sweltering long summers or in very cold polar winters.

In addition, imbalance in the neuro-vegetative system causes both an increase of activity in the parasympathetic system and excessive discharge in the stomach and in gastrin hormones. As a result, the stomach begins to develop ulcers. Changes in the neuro-vegetative system usually occur during autumn. Since the beginning of the month of Ramadan retrogresses from year to year fasting during different seasons of the year is quite fitting for those with ulcer pains related to an empty stomach.

Certain foods and fruits are consumed in certain seasons. By fasting during different seasons, the body prepares itself for the shortage of all types of food. This in turn, strengthens its resistance to many different illnesses. As it is known, some illnesses do not go together with certain types of food. For example, hot, bitter, and sour foods like pickles and spices do not have good effect on certain skin diseases. Also, allergic illnesses do not tolerate certain food intake.

Consequently, fasting at different times and seasons help the body develop endurance and immunity towards certain illnesses. When we consider the fact that the digestive system works throughout the entire human life, health benefits of resting this system, each year, at least for a month cannot be questioned.

Besides the many benefits obtained from fasting one month a year, we cannot overlook the significant effects it has on preventative health.

iii. A month of change in regular diet

During the month of fasting, the body tries to adapt to the change in regular diet. This adaptation process strengthens its resistance to ailments. It also enables the system to benefit more efficiently from the foods it consumes. Fasting allows people to work with a lighter body during the day and provides a good night's rest. Moreover, the patience and endurance displayed during the fast helps the individual to think more clearly because most of the body's blood was utilized by the brain, not the intestines. When we consider the perspective of evaluating matter according to its value and approaching life and its events with a clear mind, we realize the importance of fasting more than ever.

d. Medical Benefits of Fasting

Fasting has an effect on all faculties of the body, and it possesses health enhancing qualities. However, if a person observes the fast for health purposes only, it won't be accepted as worship. Fasting must be observed to please God. Only then will the worshipper benefit from its blessings in the shape of divine wisdom.

i. Nervous System

Due to the significant reduction in food intake, a person who observes the fast also abstains from unnecessary exhaustion without even realizing it. At the same time, every individual, depending on his financial situation, consumes considerable amount of nutrition and vitamins at *iftar* and *sahur*. Moreover, due to the break given to sexual desires, the entire nervous system begins to function healthier. The apprehensive behavior observed on some people during the fast has nothing to do with the nervous system. It is a psychological condition related to the carnal-self.

During the fast, the liver breaks down all the toxins, saving the nervous system from a significant problem we call fatigue.

ii. Blood Circulation System

When fasting, the cholesterol levels of the body drop during the day. Cholesterol deposits that have been collected in the arteries begin to break up and mix into the main blood stream. Gradually, this process relieves the hardening of blood vessels. Also, in the afternoon blood pressure drops slightly, allowing for a perfect rest at the end of the day. In a day of fasting, the body is protected from a horrific condition called "arteriosclerosis" (blockage that causes stroke).

I have personally conducted blood pressure experiments on three hundred elderly persons who fast and perform ablution on a regular basis and found no signs of arteriosclerosis. I was amazed by the fact that none of those who were over the age of 65 had blood pressure exceeding 120.

In regards to the heart, there are three issues that have negative effect on the heart: stiff arteries, neurological fatigue, and constant pressure exerted by the stomach. These three issues are automatically diminished during the fast.

iii. Digestive System

The digestive system that needs to work from birth to death receives a rest during the day until sunset throughout the fast of the month of Ramadan. Essentially, it gets an opportunity to repair its worn out components.

The most obvious health benefit of fasting is experienced in the liver. The liver has hundreds of different functions connected to the various parts of the body. All types of chemical reactions—from synthesizing the solution that enables digestion to producing the blend that protects the body from illnesses—are done in the liver. Medical disorders in the liver are rare, and when they occur it fails to perform some of its duties. Modern science believes that the starting point of most illnesses is the liver because it fails to support the immune system. Fasting enables the liver to have a break at

least 3-4 hours a day. The liver does not actually stop working, but its load is decreased during the fast, so like the other
organs, the liver also gets the opportunity to rest and renew
itself. As a result, the body's defense equipment, digestion
tool, and blood laboratory transforms into an ideal system.
This is exactly what the term, "fasting provides health relief"
means…

iv. Blood Chemistry

The initial chemical reactions of the body occur in the blood.
Various nutrients, immune system properties, and respiratory enzymes are reproduced in the blood. When there is an
increase in the numbers of these properties, the body displays
great struggle to keep up. In people who are observing the
fast, these properties remain at minimum level. As a result,
the chemical reactions in the blood occur with ease. Those
who do not observe the fast because they have weak bodies
do not realize that abstaining from fasting aggravates their
condition. The reason for this is skinny and weak bodies usually show signs of imbalance in blood chemistry.

v. Urogenital System

Without doubt, a calm nervous system and a diet controlling
the sexual desires has important effects on sexual life.

When we consider the role of the kidneys that filter the
burned-off food products, we realize the importance of the
four hours of rest that the fasting person receives during a
day of fasting. It is as if the protection of human health was
assigned to fasting hence it was bestowed upon humanity as
an obligation by the Almighty God.

e. Fasting and Psychology

Experiments conducted on students who are about to sit for life-changing exams have shown that fasting has positive effects on psychological conditions such as nervousness, anxiety, tension, and pressure.

Psychological disorders are caused by many incidents such as anxieties, shocks, stress, and fear. These conditions can erupt in situations like exams, competitions, wars, and tribunals. Blood rushing to the face and the eyes, trembling and shaking, and speech problems are symptoms of physiological disorders that are caused by hormonal and inner gland dysfunctions. According to medical research, in such situations, the adrenaline levels in some people raise drastically leading to a high sugar disorder we call diabetes. Depending on the duration of anxiety, fear or violence, the emergence of sugar diabetes may be a light, temporary condition or a severe, permanent disorder.

A certain amount of glucose is always detected in the urine of people who face horrific situations. Doctors advise people to tackle such situations with an empty stomach. This means fasting. It has been observed that fasting increases the body's resistance and endurance towards sudden shocks, fears, anxiety, and nervous tension. It develops courage and enhances effort. Fasting also regulates hormonal discharges. It calms the nerves down during psychological mood changes and prevents further harm. Fasting clears the mind and provides serenity.

Indeed, during the most challenging moments of our life, especially in situations when we face life threatening situations, it is imperative to keep calm and have our both feet on the ground. In order to display courage and sacrifice in such situations, we need to strengthen our psychology and spiritual state of mind. History records that Muslims were running to their deaths even in the fiercest of battles. Fasting played a great role in this behavior, along with a yearning to attain life's biggest trophy, martyrdom.

f. Fasting Is a Shield

The stimulation and provocation of animalistic feelings and sexual emotions depends on the amount and severity of sexual hormones. This is proportional to the effect of these hormones on the genital organs. Sexual emotions are stimulated by an increase of sexual hormones in the blood. And this increase is closely related to eating.

Fasting lowers the levels of these hormones in the blood. The serenity and calmness experienced during the fast is connected to this decrease. The fasting person develops spiritual feelings and elevation by suppressing and restraining his animalistic feelings and temptations.

The effect of fasting on sexual desires was described by the noble Prophet, "Youth who have the means to do so, should perform marriage. Those who do not possess the means should fast because fasting is a protective shield." The noble Prophet's advice to those youth who live through the toughest struggle against the dangerous waves of sexual desires and to those who wish to protect their integrity, health, and chastity has been endorsed by modern science.

g. Fasting from a Perspective of Intellectual Ability

The brain is the most amazing organ in the human body. The living tissues and cells that make up the brain form the most sensitive and organized region in the human body. These tissues and cells are connected to every nerve in the body. Ascribed with a specific duty each brain cell performs its duty with precision. With extreme care and order, it controls the functions of certain organs or regions in the body. The Almighty has bestowed more duty and endurance upon these cells than any other living tissue.

Since brain cells work two or three times more than the others, they need more blood. The weight and volume of the brain may be quite small, but it is never satisfied for blood.

One-fourth of the body's blood is used by the brain. This small organ is connected to large arteries. When the brain enters into deep contemplation, the muscles become flexed. This is an indication of hunger because the food in the stomach has been processed. In such case, most of the food has been utilized by the brain.

Since amongst living beings, humans were blessed with an ability to think through the intellect, their brains are configured differently from other life forms on earth. The amount of components that enable human beings to think is more than the entire human population!

The intellectual thinking capability of this unique organ bestowed upon human beings depends on the amount of blood it receives. This means, the more blood it receives, the better it functions. As the amount of blood decreases, it becomes indolent and begins to die out.

When the digestive organs are filled with food, most of the blood is used by them, so the brain does not receive sufficient blood. Blood deficiency renders the brain weak. When brain cells fail to work efficiently, this reflects upon the body. For this reason, after a full meal, we feel loose, our thoughts become cloudy and our bodies become slothful. As a result we feel like sleeping. This is more evident in those who overeat and continue to overindulge themselves even after meals.

Fasting has significant impact on brain cells because during the observation of the fast they receive more blood. In turn, the brain becomes more active and dynamic.

As sexual desires blind the brain, overeating, which is closely related to overindulging sexual impulse, impoverishes the brain as it affects its ability to think.

Fasting helps the brain to function better and supports the mind when facing difficult situations. In solving difficult and complex problems for which a substantial amount of thinking is needed and prior to taking important exams, one should embrace the fast.

Students who observe the fast on the day of exam will increase their ability to think and to solve problems. Their comprehension will be enhanced, their memory will flourish, their minds will be fresh, and their ability to understand will improve.

h. Fasting and Servanthood

The Almighty, with His matchless bounties, has transformed the world into a table of banquet. As He proves His Mercy and Compassion through the countless bounties He has bestowed upon us, He also proves His Lordship by timely sending sustenance to the trillions of living cells that make up the human body. Such Lordship and Mercy should be acknowledged with gratitude and worship. Yet, human beings fail to see this veiled reality and sometimes through forgetfulness or negligence, they become reluctant towards their duties of servanthood.

Indeed during the month of Ramadan, Muslims observing the fast transform into a disciplined army. In particular, as the time of *iftar* approaches, they display total submission of servanthood as they wait for the commandment to eat. With their harmonious servanthood and behavior, they display gratitude and respect towards the infinite mercy and immeasurable compassion. Would anyone who considers himself as a human being refrain from participating in such servanthood?

i. Fasting and Gratitude

God's bounties require gratitude. This is an issue that many Qur'anic verses have addressed: *"Do they not show gratitude yet?"* (Ya.Sin 36:35) *"Amongst My servants, those who show gratitude are small in numbers"* (Saba 34:13). *"But, are you being thankful?"* (Anbiya 21:80). *"Verily Allah is full of bounty to humankind, but most of them are ungrateful"* (Yunus 10:60). *"Small are the thanks that you give!"* (Araf 7:10). *"Nor will you find, in most of them, gratitude"* (Araf 7:17). *"Most of them are ungrateful"* (Baqara 2:243).

The ungratefulness of mankind has been pointed out significantly in Surah Rahman with a verse that is repeated 31 times: *"Then which of the favors of your Lord will you deny?"*

Gratefulness to the Almighty can only be displayed through acknowledgement, appreciation, and realization of need for the bounties bestowed by Him.

Fasting during Ramadan is the key to the manifestation of a pure, genuine, grand, and universal gratitude. The reason for this is that in other times, people who do not experience hunger do not realize the importance and significance of the blessings. This is more evident amongst the wealthy and the fortunate. Without doubt, at the time of *iftar*, the taste buds of all Muslims bear witness to the preciousness of a piece of bread. From a king to those who live in poverty, everyone realizes the value of God's bounties and display their gratefulness in a unique way. Moreover, by abstaining from food during the day, they acknowledge that those blessings and bounties do not belong to them; they are gifts from the true Bestower: "Now, I wait for His command in appreciation and gratitude." From this perspective, fasting becomes the key to many aspects of human gratefulness.

j. Fasting and Society

Human beings are created with different levels of financial means. For this reason, the Almighty invites the wealthy to help the needy. However, the wealthy can only comprehend and grasp the heart-breaking conditions that the needy struggle through by experiencing hunger and starvation themselves.

Without fasting, some selfish wealthy individuals would not comprehend the extreme difficulties endured by the needy and how much compassion they need. People who have full stomachs will not show empathy towards those who are starving unless they experience the feeling by refraining from food themselves. Therefore, fasting is the most suitable way to learn this kind of empathy.

Tackling the issue from this perspective, empathy towards fellow human beings is the essence of genuine gratitude. No matter how poor you are, there will always be someone poorer. Therefore, you are responsible of displaying compassion to that person. Unless individuals become obligated to experience hunger, they will not fulfill the responsibility of helping others. Even if they did, it would not be complete because they would not be able to feel their suffering.

k. The Carnal Soul Desires Freedom

The carnal soul wishes to be free and assumes that it has total freedom. Moreover, it may go to the extent by making the same claim voiced by the pharaoh, "*I am your Supreme Lord*" (Naziat 79:24). This means it imagines a false Lordship in itself. The carnal soul will not contemplate the countless bounties through which it is being assessed. Especially, if it possesses a substantial amount of wealth on earth, with the aid of somnolence, it will swallow the divine bounties just like a thieving animal as the Qur'an describes: "*They eat (God's bounties) like animals*" (Muhammad 47:12).

Indeed, during the holy month of Ramadan every carnal soul realizes that it is not the ruler but the servant, and it is a slave not a king. Without permission, it cannot even reach for a glass of water; it does not have the freedom to do as it wishes, so its imaginary lordship is shattered, and it assumes the mind-set of servanthood and displays gratefulness.

l. Fasting and Moral Education

The human carnal-self forgets its own essence through somnolence. It fails to see its own infinite weakness and poverty, so it does not confess to mistakes and errors. It does not contemplate on its own vulnerability to mortality and countless dilemmas. Moreover, it does not realize that it is made up of flesh and blood which would eventually decay and decompose. The carnal-self assumes that it is made up of steel and is immortal. Therefore, it attacks everything on earth as if it would never die. With incredible voracity and gluttony, it embraces the world with passion. It attaches itself to every pleasure and benefit. In addition, it forgets the compassionate hand of the Creator. It fails to remember the consequences of its actions and its accountability in the Hereafter. As a result, it continues to live a selfish life.

The obligatory fast observed during Ramadan reminds even the most wretched souls of their vulnerability, weakness, and poverty. Due to hunger, the carnal-self thinks about its stomach and realizes its need. It remembers the weakness and frailty of its own body. It comprehends how much it is in need of love and compassion. Therefore, it develops the feeling of refraining from pharaoh-like desires and seeks to take refuge in God as it prepares to knock on the door of mercy with his spiritual hand of gratitude. This is inevitable, if the heart is not ruined by somnolence…

m. Fasting and Qur'an

"Ramadan is the (month) in which was sent down the Qur'an, as a guide to mankind, also clear

(signs) for guidance and judgment (between right and wrong)" (Baqara 2:185).

Since the holy Qur'an was revealed in Ramadan, in order to welcome this divine announcement accordingly, we need to wait for the time of its revelation by refraining from abase requirements of the carnal-self; by abstaining from useless acts; by behaving like angels and refraining from food and drink; and by listening and reciting the holy Qur'an as if it were being revealed at that moment. Perhaps to experience that sanctified sensation, we need to listen to it as if it were being recited by the noble Prophet or by the angel Gabriel or perhaps by the Eternal Original Speaker Himself. Moreover, during this holy month, one needs to be the translator and reader of the Qur'an to others to convey the divine reason of its revelation.

Indeed, during Ramadan, perhaps the world of Islam transforms into a great mosque. This is such a great mosque that millions of *hafiz*es, or memorizers of the Qur'an, recite the Word of God at the corners of this great mosque as they broadcast its heavenly announcement to the people of the world. Each Ramadan reflects the radiant and brilliant light of the verse, *"Ramadan is a month in which the Qur'an was revealed"* (Baqara: 185). The other members of this amazing community listen to the recitations of the *hafiz* with tranquility and serenity. Some recite it to themselves. Just imagine how ugly it would be to abandon such a sanctified mosque to follow the desires of the carnal-self by eating and drinking. Such behavior would obviously draw the resentment of the believers in the mosque, just as opposing people who fast during Ramadan would draw the spiritual revulsion and disgust of the entire world of Islam.

n. Fasting and Rewards of the Hereafter

The Ramadan fast, in regards to human beings who have come to this world for trading and farming purposes, has many divine purposes, and one of the most important rewards of fasting is this: during Ramadan spiritual rewards for worship and servanthood are increased from one to a thousand. According to a hadith, reciting one letter of the holy Qur'an brings ten rewards; it earns ten fruits in Paradise. During Ramadan, each letter offers not ten but a thousand rewards and verses such as *Ayatu'l-Kursiyy* brings thousands of rewards...This is said to increase even more during the Fridays of Ramadan. The rewards increase to thirty thousand on the Night of Qadr. According to the verse, *"The Night of Qadr is more blessed than a thousand months"* (Qadr 97:3). This means thirty thousand days. Indeed, the holy Qur'an that supplies thirty thousand eternal fruits with each of its letters transforms into an eternal tree of Tuba which provides millions of spiritual fruits to believers during the holy month of Ramadan. Then come, observe and think of the sanctified, profitable, and eternal trade offered here and comprehend the extent of the deficit suffered by those who do not understand the value of these holy letters...

The month of Ramadan is actually a trading bazaar and a profitable marketplace where people can make dealings for the Hereafter. During Ramadan, the increasing and growing of worship and the rewards for these acts are like April showers. It is also an official march, a holy celebration performed by servants before the exalted sovereignty of the eternal King. For this reason, the carnal-self was ordered to observe the fast so that it refrains from useless occupations and abase animalistic requirements, such as eating and drinking and carnal temptations that it desires so much.

Perhaps, the carnal-self temporarily abandons its animalistic form and assumes an angelic one as it deals in business regarding the Hereafter. By temporarily abstaining from worldly necessities it assumes the form of a spiritual being who observes the fast as he reflects the name *as-Samad*, or the Eternally-Besought-of-All, like a spiritual mirror.

Indeed, the holy month of Ramadan contains an everlasting joy within this short transient realm and life and also provides an opportunity to earn eternal life.

Without question, one month of Ramadan can provide the opportunity to earn eighty years of life's rewards. The evidence is in the Qur'an which informs us that the Night of Qadr is equal to one thousands months of blessing.

Just as a king who declares certain days of the year as a festival to celebrate his rule or some other significant event that signifies his lordship and then invites his loyal subjects to his court for this special occasion to benefit from his compliments and amazing works and exceptional favors, so has the Sultan of eternity and infinity who is the exalted King of the eighteen thousand realms revealed His noble decree, the holy Qur'an during Ramadan. Obviously, declaring Ramadan as a special divine festival, a Godly exhibition and as a spiritual gathering is part of His divine wisdom.

Since Ramadan is such a significant celebration, certainly fasting will be ordered so that His loyal servants refrain from abase animalistic acts. The most perfect of fasting is the one in which the observer fasts with his eyes, ears, heart, imagination, and emotions just as he does with his stomach. This means refraining from all forms of religious prohibitions and useless acts by fasting with all senses and emotions. For example, keeping the tongue away from lies, slander, and cursing by giving it duties such as reciting the Qur'an, remembering God, repeating His exalted Names, repenting and offering greetings (*salawat*) to the noble Prophet, all of these may be considered as fasting observed by the tongue.

Other organs of the body can be made to fast also. For instance, the eyes can be protected from gazing at the forbidden, and the ears can be blocked to all words of evil. Instead, the eyes could observe God's creation with wisdom, and the ears could listen to religious advice and to the recitation of the holy Qur'an.

In any case, the stomach is like a huge factory and when it receives a break from work, it is easier for smaller workstations to follow suit during the fast.

o. Fasting and Patience

Fasting is the best method of physical and spiritual dieting, and it is a medical remedy. When the carnal human desire eats and drinks as it wishes, not only does it generate medical problems for the physical body, but by swallowing everything without distinguishing between lawful (*halal*) and unlawful (*haram*), it also poisons the spiritual life. Such a carnal-self will not submit to the will of the heart and soul. Like an outlaw, it will take control of the reins. From that point on, you cannot mount it, but it will mount you. During the holy month of Ramadan, it will get used to the notion of dieting through fasting. It will learn obedience and self-control. Therefore, it will not overload the poor stomach with more than it could handle. This will also keep it safe from attracting many illnesses. Since it learns to abstain from even what is normally *halal*, the practice helps it to develop an ability to abstain from *haram*. This means that one who abstains from even the *halal* during the fast, can easily abstain from *haram*. As a result, the spiritual life is not damaged.

A large number of the human population faces starvation through many forms of disasters, such as earthquakes, fire, flood, war, and poverty. In order to endure and show patience in such situations, the human body needs training and discipline. This means that the body needs to be prepared for famine and starvation. The Ramadan fast is an endurance training that lasts for an average of fifteen hours (24 hours without the predawn meal of *sahur*) every day for an entire month. This means that the Ramadan fast is a remedy for the ailments of impatience and lack of endurance.

Patience and endurance play a great role in self-development. Our physical and spiritual structures are connected to each other. Both sides can be influenced by the other. A person who can resist physical pleasures can also endure spiritual pressures. We do not even need a psychological experiment to prove this. Our ancestors who resisted the attacks of the crusaders for many centuries and under extreme circumstances are the best examples of this. Today, when we mention the world wars, we think of intolerable circumstances. Yet these battles took place between forces that were approximately equal in numbers. However, during the crusades, a coalition of more than twenty states joined forces to attack one nation, the Ottomans. By God, what kind of a resistance was this?

Acts repeated on the human body will eventually turn into habits. Habits, in turn, will transform into character and nature. Those who possess the ability to show endurance to starvation will not be destroyed by famine. This reality has been explained by Ibn Haldun, the great Islamic scholar who lived many centuries ago: "It has been observed that those who live in prosperity and abundance die more rapidly during the years of food-shortage compared to those who live in poverty. The stomachs and abdomens of people who live in abundance, especially those who eat oily food, collect more fat than the usual natural amount. When these individuals do not find oily and fatty foods and have to live with dry hardened foods, their intestines begin to dry and shrivel rapidly. Intestines are feeble organs hence diseases can penetrate them quite easily, and this may lead to a condition that causes fatality.

In situations of famine, people do not die of starvation, but rather the lack of abundance of food that they have been used to consuming. On the other hand, people who are used to consuming little food and small amounts of fats will preserve the natural fatty structure of their body. Therefore, the intestines will accept all forms of natural food. When these kinds of people change their diets, their intestines do not go through abnormality and do not dry up.

Doctors claim that 'hunger is a killer.' Their concern should be interpreted as a sudden decision to refrain from eating. Such a decision will cause complications in the intestines and invite all kinds of illnesses that we fear. However, the method of the Sufis, which includes decreasing the food intake gradually, will not be detrimental. Similarly, if one decides to stop the disciplinary diet and go back to eating large amounts of food, this should also be done gradually. The lives of people who change their diets suddenly from very little food to large amounts of food are in grave danger.

The results of a disciplined diet can be observed in healthy bodies, clear minds, and improved strength." (Muqaddimah of Ibn Haldun, 222).

In reality, no one dies due to lack of sustenance. The reason for this is certain portion of the sustenance provided by the Almighty is stocked up by our bodies as fat, so much so that every living cell reserves a certain amount of sustenance as stock. This stock is reserved as precautionary sustenance for times when food is not available.

The fatty food reserves stocked by the body can last a person for forty days. There are some cases of spiritual discipline that enables a person to tolerate hunger for more than forty days. Many years ago, we have read in the newspapers that a man who was on a hunger strike in London prison have survived for seventy days without food. More recently, we read about IRA guerillas that go on hunger strikes in British prisons for long periods of time. This means those who die during food shortage do not really die of hunger if they had died before the forty days of starvation. Perhaps, the phrase, "Abandoning habits will kill you" was meant for the habit of overeating.

Those who follow the advice of the noble Prophet and live a simple life; eat modestly and observe the fast for a month each year will be protected from such dangers. The reason for this is their metabolism becomes familiar with hunger and thus use the fat reserves stocked in their cells when needed.

p. Fasting and Sensitive Feelings

The stomach factory has many workers. Moreover, many human qualities are connected to the stomach. If the carnal-self does not close the stomach factory down for a month each year, its workers and components will neglect their private duties of worship. They will be preoccupied with the stomach and as a result will fall under its domination. The other faculties of man will also be polluted by the noise and fumes of this wearying factory. The stomach will draw attention only to itself and cause the rest of the body to forget about divine duties. This is why many saints have resorted to disciplinary diet in order to reach perfection.

Through fasting in Ramadan, the workers of that factory realize that they are not created to serve the stomach only. The rest of human feelings and emotions replace the abase pleasures of the physical factory with the angelic and spiritual ecstasies of Ramadan.

For this reason, believers attain and experience various levels of spiritual and metaphysical pleasures proportional to their rank. During this holy month, the heart and soul, intellect and essence, apparent and concealed emotions become enhanced through inspiration. In contrast to the weeping of the stomach, they smile with innocence.

PHYSICAL AND SPIRITUAL ASPECTS OF FASTING

One of the conditions of fasting is intention. This means being totally aware and conscious of the task ahead, why it needs to be performed, and for what purpose it will be performed. Starvation by a coincidence or due to uncontrollable circumstances cannot be considered fasting. Fasting has physical and spiritual aspects:

i.   Fasting is a duty of servanthood, and it is a form of worship that encompasses disciplining the free will. For this reason, a Muslim that fails to observe the fast for valid reasons must make up for the days they missed at a suitable time in the future. However, if the Ramadan fast is broken without any valid reason, they must compensate for the fast by making up the day that has been missed and an additional 60 days of fasting as a form of punishment for breaking the word given to God. As it is obvious, there is a difference between knowing and doing. For example, a doctor who drinks alcohol knows better than anyone that the substance is harmful to human health, yet he cannot stop himself from consuming this poison. Evidently, bad deeds are not performed only due to ignorance, but they are also the products of pathetic free will and bad habits. Those who give their wealth to gambling, murderers who struggle with their guilty conscience throughout their lives, students who abandon their education and become slaves of deceitful temptations, and people who complain about not being able to kick their bad habits such as smoking are the victims who have been deprived of this discipline of the soul and free will. A wild horse without a bit, saddle, and rein can easily cause the destruction of its owner. Fasting is a disciplinary worship that will grab the rein of our carnal-self and place it in our hands. Through fasting the carnal-self will be disciplined and will submit to the will of God. As a result, it will become an obedient broken mount. It is a fact that our environment is full of temptations and blessings that encourage our desires and entice our emotions. By means of fasting, we give our word to God that we will refrain from them for the designated period only to please Him. Consequently, we abandon our animalistic side and take a step towards becoming angelic beings that perform this duty with intention and in awareness. This in turn strengthens our free will and illuminates our heart and soul because we have exerted our efforts to please God.

ii. Every human being possesses a sense of egotism that resembles Nimrod and the Pharaoh. This egotism believes that it will never die and that it will live eternally on this earth. It tricks itself into believing that it is immortal. Now, let us take a look at a person who observes the fast. Even in a day of fasting, the light of his eyes become dimmed, his legs begin to shake from hunger, and he senses a significant decrease in his strength. Realizing that he is not all that powerful or dominant, he will acknowledge the true source of power and his weakness next to the All-Powerful God.

Fasting Serves Every Essential of Human Complexity

All human essentials, physical and spiritual, benefit from fasting. As fasting effects all living cells in our bodies, it provides relief and serenity. This is why those who observe the fast do not feel much hunger and thirst. In contrast, those who do not fast feel the pain of hunger and thirst at extreme levels when they do not eat or drink for the same period as the duration of the fast.

The term starvation should not only be understood as deprivation from food. It means abstaining from all forms of temptations. For this reason, when we list the types of obligatory worship, fasting appears on top of the list. In order to achieve a complete fast, the carnal-self must abstain from all bad habits. Diminishing moral weaknesses such as sexual desires and arrogance enables the fast to make an impact on the carnal-self. Qur'anic verses clearly indicate the various levels of fasting, pointing in particular to the above aspect.

The body's joint worship with the carnal-self on a physical platform during the fast can be defined as: withholding the tongue from foul language, turning the gaze away from the forbidden, removing the terms God forbids from the language and turning away automatically from what is religiously forbidden. Also upholding *taqwa* (fear of God) and making a habit out of it is the joint fasting performed by the carnal-self and body. The person observing the fast must protect all limbs against sins and be aware of any action that may lead to wrongful conduct. Just as he refrains from lawful food and drink while observing the fast, he must also protect his tongue against lies and foul language, hands against forbidden acts, eyes against unlawful looks, ears against listening to lies and gossip, and feet against the pursuit of bad deeds.

In regards to the soul: If it feels the pain, joy, and serenity of fasting only for the sake of God, the soul is also fasting. What this means is, pain and suffering should be embraced as pleasures, only for the sake of God.

Fasting is the reins and bit that restrain the carnal soul. It hinders man from having pharaoh-like egos. The Prophet stated that when God created the carnal-self, He asked: "Who am I and who are you?" The carnal-self replied: "You are you and I am me." God punished it in Hellfire and then asked the same question again. The reply was no different: "You are you and I am me." Finally, God punished it with starvation and then asked once again: "Who am I and who are you?" The carnal-self replied: "You are my merciful Lord, compassionate Owner and I am Your impotent subject, needy servant!"

Fasting of the heart occurs when it is filled with nothing but the love of God and His Messenger. Such a heart does not accept tips or gifts anymore, occupying itself with nothing else but God. How fortunate are those who observe the fast with these four essentials to earn the pleasure of God.

FASTING: REIN AROUND THE NECK OF THE CARNAL-SELF

Unlike the other living beings, human emotions were not restricted by boundaries. In this regard there is no limit to their evil or good deeds. The main reason for this is this world is a realm of assessment, a testing ground. So, in order to advance or regress human beings need freedom of choice. As a result, there will be those who surpass the angels and those who will plunge down to level that is lower than that of the animals.

With this in mind, Islamic principles have established certain limits for the free will so that human abilities can be improved in a positive way. If one submits to all the desires of the carnal-self, he will fall from an angelic level to the level of a beast. The representatives of civilizations based on materialism stand before our very eyes as examples. The enticing services provided by these civilizations work vigorously to satisfy the carnal desires of the flesh by making them easier to obtain. This leads to a selfish, dissolute lifestyle. Therefore, humanity goes through a spiritual change. Even if they appear to be humans on the outside, they resemble the four-legged creatures in the inside (in manners). If we had the chance to turn some of these so-called civilized individuals inside-out, we would behold the reflections of such creatures as the monkey, fox, snake, bear, and swine. Their furry and hairy images will appear before us. And if we had the opportunity to visit the headquarters of some of these individuals, we would see scorpions wearing human clothes and demons appearing in human form.

Indeed, when human emotions and desires are not restricted by the required limitations, we end up with the picture of humanity we observe today. Sexual desires and carnal temptations must be disciplined and taught to obey orders. Fasting is the most perfect system to achieve this because fasting offers the most practical method of controlling the carnal-self. If evil desires are controlled and kept under pressure, they will not take over the human being.

BIOCHEMICAL RESEARCH CONDUCTED ON THE ISLAMIC FAST

The committee of scientists who have conducted the research includes:

Prof. M. Münip Yeğin, Dr. Mustafa Ünal, Dr. Turhan Soysal, Specialist Dr. Abdülkadir Usta, Specialist Dr. M. Yaşar Çil, Dr. Selma Çekirdek, Specialist Dr. Ekin Önder, Specialist Dr. Gökhan Timuralp, Specialist Pharmacist Vedat Akın, Specialist Chemist Zeki Arı, Specialist Chemist Ebubekir Bakan, Specialist Chemical Engineer Serpil Tuncel, Dr. Hüseyin T. Sessiz, Dr. Bülent Akpınar.

Introduction

The paper we will present here is the annalistic study of the biochemical blood chart during the Islamic fast. There are two reasons for selecting this topic: in recent years a number of papers regarding the preventative health benefits of fasting have been published.

a. Some of these papers cover health complications such as arteriosclerosis, high blood pressure, obesity, infarctus, angina pectoris, and high cholesterol symptoms.

b. Many of our students and people from the community have brought forward a number of questions in relation to this topic.

Overeating does not increase our strength; on the contrary, it causes a loss of strength. In addition, it has a devastating effect on our budgets. There are three main reasons for this:

1. All types of excessive food deposits take up unnecessary space in our digestive channel and in our internal

organs preventing our cells from performing their duties efficiently whilst distorting their balanced diet.

2. In order to protect itself from the detrimental effects of excessive food, the body decreases the functions of the organs in the digestive channel. This in turn attracts certain disorders such as constipation, obesity, rheumatism, arteriosclerosis and probably cancer that target the liver, kidneys, stomach, and the intestines.

3. In order to dissolve the excessive food that enters the body, the components of the digestive system begin to produce liters of digestive liquids and enzymes and use a significant amount of energy to neutralize and expel these substances from the body without even using them.

A summary of the argument

Non-Islamic fasting has provided the following results:

a. During the initial days of fasting, there is an increase in blood and urinal urea.

b. The increase in urea indicates to breaking of proteins in the body, which means a decrease in the number of proteins in the blood.

c. During the four weeks of fasting the percentage of glycemia (blood-sugar) does not drop below 80% mg. However, in the fifth week it drops to 75% mg.

d. The levels of free fatty acids increase and this indicates lipid break downs.

e. There is also a decrease in amino acids in the blood; this is due to rapid gluconeogenesis.

f. The level of ketones increases in the blood. Therefore, the body has expelled a significant amount of acetone with the urine.

g. There is significant weight loss during total starvation.

Studies conducted on 100 people observing the Islamic fast and results obtained from 54 subjects in relation to the points listed above are as follows:

a. There is no urea increase in the blood.

b. There is no protein decrease in the blood.

c. The levels of glycemia have only dropped down to 83.91% mg.

d. The free fatty acids have not increased; rather there is a decrease in the amount.

e. The number of amino acids in the blood has increased.

f.   Acetone has not been detected in the urine.

g. Weight loss in the Islamic fasting is so insignificant that we can conclude there is no weight loss.

Conclusion

Our research was conducted in modern labs and yielded the below results:

1. Physiological starvation was not detected in the Islamic way of fasting.

2. We can assume that Islamic fasting quickens the lipid metabolism within physiological limits by activating the fat deposits in the body. This reduces the possibility of developing arteriosclerosis.

3. The Islamic way of fasting is a perfect method of "Medical Prophylaxis" or preventative health that protects the

observer from a number of modern age health complaints such as atherosclerosis and its partners, like high cholesterol, hypertension, angina pectoris, infarctus, and some kidney disorders that are common among those living in comfort.

4. The hunger experienced during the Islamic fast comes from prohibition of habitual eating, thus it can be defined as "psychological hunger" or "phantom hunger".

5. The Islamic fast is an effective treatment for illnesses except some rare conditions.

6. Since Islamic fasting cannot be regarded as starvation, we can say that it is a type of "holistic diet".

This research was conducted on 100 subjects from various occupations, 84 males and 16 females between the ages of 18–65. Blood samples were taken and analyzed from the subjects prior to and in the last week of Ramadan. In addition to this, another 54 subjects, between the ages of 10–47 (42 males and 12 females) were weighed during the last week of Ramadan and a month after the conclusion of Ramadan.

The analytic data obtained from the research suggests that there is a significant difference between the characteristics of starvation and the Islamic fast. It was established that Islamic fasting is a preventative health method. It works by mobilizing the fat deposits in the body to address modern complaints that rise from wealthy lifestyle and comfort.

Note: The above abstract was the brief summary of the original research.

CHAPTER III

Zakat, the Obligatory Alms

ZAKAT (PRESCRIBED PURIFYING ALMS)

Zakat is the most perfect alms giving system that protects human beings from the disease of parsimony; it saves people from degrading poverty and begging; it protects the society from sedition, rebellion, and crime; it protects the very structure of social life and prevents the eruption of civil wars; and it reminds human beings that the true owner of all wealth is the Almighty God. Zakat also serves as an important tool in the spreading of Islam as it enables people who receive the alms to warm up to Islam. Zakat also helps to spread Islam through struggle. Certainly, those who serve Islam and spend their life in the way of spreading God's name should not be concerned of financial hardship or difficulties of daily living. They should be supported so that they can serve Islam freely and wholeheartedly.

The Prescribed Purifying Alms (the *Zakat*) are meant only for the poor, and the destitute (albeit, out of self-respect, they do not give the impression that they are in need), and those in charge of collecting (and administer-

ing) them, and those whose hearts are to be won over
(for support of God's cause, including those whose hostility is to be prevented), and to free those in bondage
(slavery and captivity), and to help those over-burdened
with debt, and in God's cause (to exalt God's word, to
provide for the warriors and students, and to help the
pilgrims), and for the wayfarer (in need of help). This is
an ordinance from God. God is All-Knowing, All-Wise.
(Tawba 9:60)

There are social, economic, and worship aspects of zakat.
By giving zakat, the believer fulfils his/her obligation to God
and concedes that all wealth belongs to Him. On the other
hand, zakat plays an important role in livening up the economy, in establishing social justice, and in forming social
cohesion amongst the members of society.

A believer submits to God in all issues of life. The evidence of this submission in regards to economic life is giving
zakat for the sake of God to those designated by Him.

It is to be noted that the rulings and decrees of the Qur'an
come from perpetuity hence they will go to eternity. They do
not age and die like human civil laws. They remain young
and powerful. For example, laws and regulations of human
civilization, their doctrines and education systems, morals
and ethics and their charitable organizations cannot compete
against the two decrees of the holy Qur'an. These two
decrees are, *"And be steadfast in Prayer; practice regular charity"* (Baqara 2: 43) and *"God has permitted trade and forbidden
usury"* (Baqara 2:275). These two essentials have kept the
religious and social lives on their feet. The reason for this is
that the daily prayers remind us of God's greatness and glory;
they also confirm that He has infinite knowledge and that He

is aware of everything we do, so He has the power to hold us accountable for our acts. The daily prayers also influence life by remaining in our minds as a preventative of evil deeds. They encourage the intellect to ever turn to God and form a feeling of obedience that leads to submission to God's commandments. Since human beings need to live in societies, in order to establish their private and social lives, they need divine laws. People and societies that do not embrace such a beneficial thing as the daily prayers or abandon them due to indolence face great loss. As "prayers are the main pillar of religion", "zakat is the bridge of Islam." With these two hadiths, the noble Prophet indicates that prayers protect the religion and zakat protects social harmony. Indeed, Muslims can only support each other by passing over the bridge of zakat. Therefore, zakat is the main vehicle of charity. It is a bridge that controls social harmony and establishes public order. In the human world, in order to achieve social harmony we need social support. Social support and charity is the essential medicine that cures catastrophes like rebellion, insurgency, conflicts, and insubordination.

SOCIAL ASPECTS OF ZAKAT

Zakat Cures Social Diseases and Liberates Society from Interest

Certainly, there is divine wisdom, a great benefit, and mercy in making zakat an obligatory act and forbidding usury and interest. Indeed, if you browse through the pages of history, and observe the evil that has stained those pages, and if you concentrate on the errors and mistakes made by humanity, you will realize that all rebellions, seditions, and wicked behavior have originated from two phrases:

The first phrase: "As long as my stomach is full, I do not care if others die of starvation!"

The second phrase: "You work vigorously so I could benefit from these bounties in comfort; you work, I'll eat; you provide the labor, and I'll consume."

Zakat is the only method that will save humanity from the first mentality that brings humanity almost to the brink of social implosion.

The abolishment of usury (interest) is the only thing that could protect humanity from the second notion that aims to destroy the society by pushing it into the abyss of social unrest.

One of the most important essentials of protecting social harmony is removing the gaps between the members of the society. The distance between the upper class and the lower class, the wealthy and the poor should not be opened. It should always remain close enough to enable interaction. Interaction between different levels of society can only be achieved through zakat and other Islamic methods of social support. Unfortunately, because they do not fulfill the obligation of zakat and carry on in dealing with usury, the gap between the wealthy and the poor continues to grow. Therefore, the connection has been broken. This is why instead of love, obedience, and respect, the only sound that rises from the bottom to the top is the chanting of vengeance, hatred, grudge, and resentment. In reply, instead of caring, sharing, and compassion, there is tyranny, despotism, oppression, and accusation raining down from the top.

Alas, when the qualities of the upper class should be modesty and compassion, they have become arrogance and conceit. On the other hand, poverty necessitates charity, assistance, and care; however these days, it brings slavery and humiliation. Take a good look at the nations of the world today; they stand as evidence to our argument...

The Islamic principles of zakat (prescribed purifying alms) and sadaqa (the voluntary alms) are the only way that societies can establish solid bonds between the lower and the upper class. Therefore, social harmony and peace can only be achieved by implementing these principles as essential legislations.

Social Cohesion

Historically, there is no rebellious group of starving people in any part of Islamic history. The history of Islam does not have incidents like the ones occurred during the French Revolution. Unfortunately, when the feelings of compassion were burned off from the souls of Muslims, we began to experience social diseases which we had caught from the French just like the contagious disease of syphilis.

Social harmony is the most important component in the existence and continuation of society. Essentially, this rests on mutual love. As a matter of fact, the universe we live in is in order. The tiniest particles of the universe are connected to each other with forces of attraction. This means that divine love manifests even in inanimate matter. With divine love, God has bonded the components of the entire universe through a general force we call gravitation. The manifestation of this divine love occurs differently in the hearts of individuals and societies. In human societies, initial love between different communities or groups is attained through mutual support. Even in poorest societies, zakat given from one-fortieth of the wealth and *ushr* (cultivation charity) given from one-tenth of the crops will generate improvement in the economy. With the light of love, each member of the society will become the other's friend. Communism, which was a horrid retaliation caused by the gaps between the wealthy and poor members of society, has crumbled under the zakat and charity institutions of the Islamic economy. In conclusion, this is the only way that a friendship could be established between the poor and the wealthy. Only then can a healthy and harmonious society be achieved.

ZAKAT AND ECONOMY

Freezing and stockpiling goods is not a healthy business practice. On the contrary, they should be put to work. As an implementation, zakat puts this in order. If the capital owner does not put his capital to work, his assets will lose one-fortieth of its value each year through zakat. The reason for this is: Zakat is a right collected from the capital not from the profits. In this case, in order to protect his assets, the capital owner will invest them in business. So, the institute of zakat encourages the economy by bringing activity to dead capital. Verses 34–35 of the Surah at-Tawba states: *"Those who hoard up gold and silver and do not spend it in God's cause (to exalt His cause and help the poor and needy): give them (O Messenger) the glad tidings of a painful punishment. On that day, that hoarded wealth will be heated in the fire of Hell and therewith their foreheads and their sides and their backs will be branded (and they will hear): 'This is the treasure which you hoarded up for your-selves; taste now what you were busy hoarding!'"* Also the 7th verse of Surah al-Hashr cautions the wealthy: *"In order that it (gold and silver) may not (merely) make a circuit between the wealthy among you."* This verse declares clearly that the wealth should not be a means of prosperity circulated among the rich only. Indeed, hoarding up money and goods without spending them in the way of God to promote God's cause and to help the poor and needy is one of the major sins.

Since capital is merely capital, it does not have the right to earn a profit. In addition, besides its possessor, others also have rights upon it. *"And in their wealth the poor (who had to beg) and the destitute (who did not beg out of shame) had due share (a right they gladly honored)"* (Dhariyat 51:19). For this reason, capital earns the right to make a profit only when it is invested in trade where it could gain or lose. For example: in a two-party business partnership in which one party comes up with the capital and the other party works, the capital provider earns the right to a profit due to the risk of losing his entire capital. Same principles apply to all situations where the capital is put to work.

COLLECTION OF ZAKAT

"The Prescribed Purifying Alms (the Zakat) are meant only for the poor, and the destitute (albeit, out of self-respect, they do not give the impression that they are in need), and those in charge of collecting (and administering) them..." (Tawba 9:60). This verse indicates that it is the very duty of an Islamic administration to establish an independent body for the collection of zakat. Furthermore, the salaries of those who work for this official body

should be provided from the collected zakat. It is the duty of the government to collect all forms of zakat and to distribute them accordingly. Islam has given extensive authority to the government in relation to collection of zakat. The collection of zakat is so imperative that if there is a powerful group who refuses to give alms, the government has the right to wage war upon them. During the time of Caliph Abu Bakr, such war was waged on those who refused to give the prescribed alms. The government has the authority to confiscate a part of the wealth of those who refuse to give alms to the administration. In a hadith, the noble Prophet states, "Whoever gives zakat with the hope of earning divine blessings shall be rewarded by God. However, we will confiscate certain part of the wealth of those who refrain from zakat because a certain part of this wealth is a right of those designated by God. No part of this is *halal* for those who come from Muhammad's lineage (Therefore, the progeny of the Prophet are equally ineligible to be zakat recipients)." Indeed, Islam has assigned the government to collect the zakat and distribute it to those designated by the Qur'an. Leaving this to individuals has its consequences. These can be summarized as:

a. The conscience of some people may have diminished due to worldly interests and pleasures. At the very least, it could become distorted and refuse to give zakat. So, leaving the rights of the needy in such hands would not be fair.

b. If the needy collect their rights from the government, instead of receiving it directly from wealthy individuals, this will protect their honor. Therefore, those in poverty would not supplicate for what is rightfully theirs.

c. Leaving zakat to individuals can also generate confusion. It is possible that many wealthy individuals may give zakat to the same needy people, and as a result, people who are less fortunate may be deprived of it.

d. Zakat is not only distributed amongst the poor, needy, and underprivileged travelers. Zakat should also be used for the common cause of the Muslim society. These causes cannot be defined by individuals. It is the duty of the government and its elite committee. Preparing teams that would work on warming people's hearts to Islam and organizing movements to spread Islam are the duties of the administration.

For all of the above reasons, the government must establish a special zakat fund, a budget where it can all be accumulated. This budget should be added as a separate fund to the general budget that would be used for various reasons.

This way, no one will be left to live under bridges. Paths to stealing will be closed and potential enemies of society will realize that they are a part of this society. Therefore, the road to anarchism will be sealed off.

The organization regarding collecting and administering zakat was managed from a single center during the time of the Prophet. The Prophet denied the request to refuse zakat payment and warned the official collectors against oppression and justice, telling the officials to "collect the zakat but avoid seizing their best possessions" and the public to be kind towards the collectors. In the past, those who refused to give zakat were sternly dealt with. Bukhari relates from Abu Hurayra: "The noble Messenger of God states, "If Allah bestows wealth upon someone and he does not give alms; on the Day of Judgment that wealth will transform into a bald snake that has two black spots above its eyes. This snake will wrap itself around the neck of its owner, squeezing him tightly as it utters, 'I am your wealth, your treasure!'" After the statement, the noble Messenger recited the following verse: *"And let not those who covetously withhold of the gifts which Allah has given them of His Grace, think that it is good for them: No, it will be the worse for them. Soon shall the things which they covetously withheld be tied to their necks like a twisted collar on the Day of Judgment. To Allah belong the heritage of the heavens and the earth, and Allah is well-acquainted with all that you do"* (Al Imran 3:180).

The punishment on earth for those who do not give zakat is explained in a hadith: "Allah will send famine and starvation upon tribes that do not give zakat" (Ibn Maja, al-Bazzar, and al-Bayhaqi). In another hadith, the noble Prophet states, "If they do not give the zakat of their wealth, they will be deprived of the rain that comes from above. They would receive no rain, if it were not for the animals" (al-Bazzar, al-Bayhaqi). Also in another hadith, the noble Prophet stated, "If zakat is mixed into the wealth, which means if it is not separated from the wealth and given to the needy, it will nullify that wealth" (Abu Dawud and Nasai). This was interpreted as God will destroy the wealth from which zakat is not given.

BENEFITS OF ZAKAT FOR THE BENEFACTOR AND RECIPIENTS

There are many divine blessings in zakat which is an obligatory act confirmed by the evidence provided by the Qur'an, Sunnah and the *Ijma* (consensus) of the ummah:

a. Giving zakat means: supporting the weak, helping those who are in hardship and assisting the underprivileged so that they could perform their obligations of faith and worship to God.

b. Zakat purifies the carnal-self of the giver from the blemishes of sin. The moral behavior of the person who gives zakat also becomes purified of parsimony and miserliness by attaining the qualities of benevolence and generosity. The carnal-self was created with a nature that behaves parsimoniously in regards to wealth. Zakat is a means to develop tolerance, and it trains one to return the entrusted goods back to its original owner. In the holy Qur'an, the Almighty states: *"Take alms (prescribed or voluntary) out of their wealth so that you (O Messenger) may thereby cleanse them and cause them to grow in purity and sincerity, and pray for them"* (Tawba 9:103).

c. The Almighty has endowed the wealthy with various bounties and possessions that surpass their requirements. They live a life of comfort as they indulge themselves in His bounties. Therefore, displaying gratefulness for God's bounties is an obligatory act, and zakat is the best form of gratitude.

d. When a person distributes his wealth, which was bestowed upon him as a blessing by God, to those in need, he acts against the wishes of his carnal-self, which in essence built on parsimony and stinginess. Therefore, the carnal-self that always inclines to evil is gradually disciplined.

e. A wealth without zakat will become *haram* (religiously forbidden). By giving zakat, this wealth is purified and becomes *halal* (religiously permitted). As a matter of fact, linguistically zakat means purification. Just as food infested with bacteria, filth, and grime would make the consumer ill, *haram* food will bring spiritual illnesses to its consumer. Spiritual and social illnesses originate from not giving zakat. To attain spiritual maturity and to illuminate the feelings and emotions of spirituality, one needs to nourish oneself with *halal* and clean sustenance provided of God. This is also imperative for social peace and serenity.

f. In accordance with the hadith that states, "Charity prolongs life," a prosperous life has strong connections with zakat. As mentioned above, one cannot think of affluence and prosperity in the lives of an ailing individual and a sick society.

g. Since the giver distributes the alms with gratitude, this zakat opens a path to the bestowal of new bounties. In the Qur'an, the Almighty God states: *"And (remember also) when your Lord proclaimed: 'If you are thankful (for My favors), I will most certainly give you more; but if you are ungrateful, surely My punishment is severe'"* (Ibrahim 14:7).

h. The person who gives zakat feels serenity, joy, and contentment in his heart and subconscious. That day, he is freed from worldly pressures, distresses of the heart, and the burden of materialism. In Western societies, some psychologists encourage their patients who are experiencing extreme depression due to heavy involvement in materialistic matters to make donations or give charity. The Almighty God rewards every good deed, initially by creating a spiritual contentment and tranquility in the hearts. This is a feeling that cannot be replaced by any materialistic means. By giving charity, the spiritual world of these patients expands and their hearts are filled with joy.

PROTECTION FROM CALAMITIES AND MISFORTUNES

As zakat brings prosperity to everyone, it also protects from calamities and misfortunes. Those who refuse to give zakat will lose that particular amount in some other way, or a disaster will take it away from their hands.

The great Islamic scholar Bediüzzaman explains an interesting dream: "It was during the fifth year of the First World War, when I was asked in an authentic dream: 'What is the purpose of this famine, poverty, and physical hardship that Muslims face today?' I replied in the dream:

'The Almighty requested that we give one-tenth of the crops such as wheat that we cultivate each year and one-fortieth of the trade products so that the prayers of the poor and the needy would be upon us and so that their grudges and resentments stay away from us. However, greed and gluttony prevented us from giving. As a result, the Almighty took eighty percent of our crops and seventy-five percent of our wealth that we had accumulated. In addition, the divine wisdom requested that we refrain from food for a month each year. We pitied ourselves and abandoned a temporary but pleasing hunger. As a punishment, the Almighty God forced us to observe a stern fast-like starvation for five years.

Also, He prescribed that we perform a prayer that took one hour out of the twenty-four hours of the day. This was a pleasant and exalted, sanctified and beneficial training for us. We displayed indolence and abstained from the daily prayers. We wasted that hour by mixing it into the others. As reimbursement, the Almighty put us through a harsh military training and enduring struggle thus forced us to perform that prayer!'"

Zakat is an essential pillar that supports the happiness and harmony of humanity. It is imperative not only for individuals or certain communities but for the continuation of the entire social life. The reason for this is that human society is made up of two levels: the upper and the lower. Zakat is the only thing that can establish the flow of compassion and mercy from the upper class and respect and compliance from the lower. Otherwise, there will be oppression and tyranny coming down from the top and insurgence and resentment rising up from the bottom. Both levels of humanity are in constant spiritual struggles and in ongoing conflicts. This will eventually lead to a major conflict between labor and capital, just as it occurred previously in Communist Russia.

CONDITIONS FOR DISBURSING CHARITY

There are certain conditions for giving zakat (prescribed alms) and sadaqa (voluntary alms):

a. Charity should not be wasted.

b. It should be given from one's own wealth not borrowed from others.

c. The blessing must not be distorted by giving with arrogance.

d. Charity must not be abandoned due to fear of poverty.

e. The receiver of the charity must spend it for his essential necessities not for pleasures.

The holy Qur'an explains the conditions and essence of charity in the third verse of Surah Baqara. It does not use terms like "They give zakat" or "They give sadaqa," but it offers comprehensive and detailed sentences such as, *"(For the sake of God) they distribute a portion from the provision. We have bestowed upon them."* The main reasons for this style of speech are:

• The term *"portion"* signified with the letter "mim" in the verse indicates that one must abstain from squander.

• According to the Qur'anic grammar, the restriction rising from passivity indicates that it must be given from one's own wealth.

• The term, *"from the provision We bestowed"* rejects arrogance when giving charity because the real bestower is God.

• Also, the indication that sustenance is given by God suggests that one should not be afraid of poverty.

• The mentioning of provision in a general sense indicates that it is not confined to the material possessions, but it includes everything that comes under the term provision like knowledge, wisdom, power, and etc.

• In the term "yunfiqun" (sustenance) indicates that the receiver should use it for essential needs, not pleasures.

The Qur'an refers to all these aspects in various verses in detail. For example:

> Those who, when they spend, are not extravagant and not niggardly, but hold a just (balance) between those (extremes). (Furqan 25:67)

> And give his due to the relative, as well as the destitute and the wayfarer; and do not squander (your wealth) senselessly. Surely squanderers are ever brothers of satans; and Satan is ever ungrateful to his Lord. (Isra 17: 26–27)

> The parable of those who spend their wealth in God's cause is like that of a grain that sprouts seven ears, and in every ear there are a hundred grains. God multiplies for whom He wills. God is All-Embracing (with His mercy), All-Knowing. Those who spend their wealth in God's cause and then do not follow up what they have spent with putting (the receiver) under obligation and taunting, their reward is with their Lord, and they will have no fear, nor will they grieve. A kind word and forgiving (people's faults) are better than almsgiving followed by taunting. God is All-Wealthy and Self-Sufficient, (absolutely independent of the charity of people), All-Clement (Who shows no haste in punishing.) O you who believe! Render not vain your almsgiving by putting (the receiver) under an obligation and taunting– like him who spends his wealth to show off to people and be praised by them, and believes not in God and the Last Day. The parable of his spending is that of a rock on which there is soil; a heavy rain falls upon it, and leaves it barren. They have no power (control) over what they have earned. God guides not such disbelieving people (to attain their goals). The parable of those who spend their wealth in pursuit of where God's good

pleasure lies and to make their hearts firmly established (in faith) is that of a garden on a hilltop: a heavy rain falls upon it, and it yields its produce twofold; even if no heavy rain falls upon it, yet a light shower suffices. Whatever you do, God sees it well. Would any of you wish to have a garden of palms and vines with rivers flowing in it, where he has all kinds of crops, and that, when old age has come upon him while he has offspring still too small (to look after their affairs), a fiery whirl-wind should smite it, and it should be burnt up? Thus does God make clear to you the Revelations (and signs of truth), that you may reflect (on them and act accordingly). (Baqara 2:261–266)

Satan frightens you with poverty and bids you into indecencies, whereas God promises you forgiveness from Himself and bounty. God is All-Embracing (with His mercy), All-Knowing. (Baqara 2:268)

Do not give to those of weak mind your property that God has put in your charge (as a means of support for you and for the needy), but feed and clothe them out of it (especially, with the profit you will make by exploiting it), and speak to them kindly and words of honest advice. (Nisa 4:5)

There is another important issue: If donations and charity are not given in the name of zakat, there are three losses. They will bring no benefit to the giver, and since it is not given in the name of God, the needy are left under the slavery of obligation. Moreover, the giver becomes deprived of the acceptable prayers of the needy. In addition, you assume that the wealth belongs to you, when in fact it belongs to the true Bestower. Therefore, you display ingratitude towards the blessings which you were obligated to distribute in any case.

When you give it as zakat, you give it in the name of God. As a result, you show gratitude from the bounties and earn divine rewards. Also, the underprivileged individual who receives it will no longer need to fawn or flatter you and demean himself. Therefore, their prayers for you will be pure and acceptable. Now, compare zakat to other methods of charity that produce hypocrisy, arrogance, conceit, humiliation, and degradation. Can any other method of charity compete with zakat that brings sincerity, compassion, performance of a religious obligation, and divine rewards?

CHAPTER IV

Hajj, the Holy Pilgrimage

HAJJ (PILGRIMAGE TO THE HOUSE OF GOD)

The worship of Hajj has two aspects: one relates to the individual and the other to social life. The individual aspect of Hajj, in particular, is quite important. Hajj is a form of worship and servanthood that is performed at the highest spiritual level. Just as a soldier appears before the king, the vizier, and the generals on the king's festive day and receives honors and compliments, similarly, the pilgrim—even if he is an average member of society—has journeyed through the ranks and like a saint, he has been elevated to the highest level to stand before the Lord of the worlds, the Almighty God. He is honored with a universal worship. Obviously, the various ranks of the universal Lordship that becomes unlocked with the key of Hajj and the exalted horizons that can only be observed through the binoculars of Hajj and the millions of believers from different races and ranks gathered by the principles of Hajj, chanting "Labbayk... Allahumma Labbayk" (which means, "Here I am, O God, at Your command! Here I am at Your command!") can satisfy the thirst, curiosity, and awe of the spiritual circle of servanthood which constantly expands as it observes the ranks and manifestations of omnipotence and listens to the chanting of "Allahu Akbar... Allahu Akbar" (God is the All-Great...God is the All-Great!) with the imagination and the heart. Through Hajj, the believer can declare and testify to the spiritual ranks that manifest in his heart or vision, his imagination or mind. After Hajj, such a profound meaning can only be found at exalted and universal levels in the Eid prayers, the prayer for rain, in the prayers performed during solar and lunar eclipses, and in the prayers performed in congregation. This is the mystery behind import of the *sha'air*, or public symbols that identify Islam and the Muslim community, even if they are in the nature of Sunnah.

The second aspect of Hajj relates to social, economical, and political lives of Muslims. Hajj is an international Muslim congregation that meets for a great affair. Let us take a brief look at some important issues regarding the matter:

1. Visiting these holy lands where Islam was born and spread and observing with our own eyes the places where the noble Messenger of God and his Companions have struggled will rejuvenate our hearts and revitalize our Islamic lives. In every step of this holy region which contains the scent of the noble Prophet and the treasures of thousands of sacred memories, there is a hidden mystery of a secret realm. In a land that has embraced so many Prophets, dying hearts will be resurrected and believers will rejoice with fresh ardor and enthusiasm.

2. Interpretation of the Qur'anic statements, in a practical living sense, can only be achieved through Hajj. *"Remember when We assigned to Abraham the site of the House (Ka'ba) as a*

place of worship, (directing him): 'Do not associate any partners with Me in any way, and keep My House pure (from any material and spiritual filth) for those who will go round it in devotion, and those who will stand in prayer before it, and those who will bow down and prostrate themselves in worship.' Publicly proclaim the (duty of) Pilgrimage for all humankind, that they come to you on foot and on lean camels, coming from every far-away point, so that they may witness all (the spiritual, social, and economic) benefits in store for them, and offer during the known, appointed days the sacrificial cattle that He has provided for them by pronouncing God's Name over them. Eat of their meat and feed the distressed, the poor. Thereafter let them tidy themselves up (by having their hair cut, removing their ihram (Hajj attire), taking a bath, and clipping their nails, etc.), and fulfill the vows (if they have made any, and complete other acts of the Pilgrimage), and go round the Most Ancient, Honorable House in devotion" (Hajj 22:26–29). These verses that bring history before our eyes, like a living page, take us back centuries to a time and place where Prophet Abraham climbed Mt. Abu Qubays and shouted: "Oh people! Perform pilgrimage to the house of your Lord!" The Almighty carries his voice even to those who are still in their father's waist and in their mother's womb. These invitations begin to flourish in the hearts of human beings, just like a seed that blossom into a flower. Believers become fascinated and engrossed by these divine cautions and invitations and turn towards the direction of the sound. Then they bow and submit to the decrees that the Lord has informed them of regarding Hajj.

3. Hajj is the remembrance of the divine memories that have become infinite. Hajj is an exhibition of masterpieces

such as Prophet Abraham and his son Ishmael, who were a nation by themselves; the last Messenger of God, Muhammad (peace and blessings be upon him), whose noble life that had attracted the envy of even those who live in the heavens; and the Companions who endured all kinds of difficulties to protect their faith on these lands. Hajj will remind us of the family that journeyed through the desert with a baby in their arms only for the sake of God; the dignified son who was ready to sacrifice his soul and the obedient father who was prepared to sacrifice his son, and a loyal mother who obeyed her husband's commandments unconditionally because she knew that he had total submission in God.

4. Expos and trade fairs are the foundation of world's economy. If we consider this as one of the many aspects of Hajj, we will realize the importance of various Muslim nations coming together on this occasion to build economic ties. Moreover, research indicates that the Arabian Peninsula contains rich resources of petrol, uranium, gold, silver, and copper. This is a region that has iron reserves sufficient until the Day of Judgment, so Muslims who visit the region each year can mutually benefit from these resources. Even if we concentrate only on petrol, the region produces 75% of the world's fuel. If Muslims took the responsibility of being concerned with the well-being of all Muslims of the world, they could easily establish an economic summit from which all Muslims of the world could benefit, and thus their rights would be protected. The divine bounties bestowed upon the *jama'ah* (group of Muslim people or Muslim society at large) are different than the ones that are given to individuals as expressed in a hadith: "The mercy of Allah is upon the

jama'ah." Indeed, each year during the Hajj season, God's mercy rains upon every *jama'ah*. If Muslims act upon divine wisdom and mercy, these bounties will enable the world of Islam to live in prosperity and affluence.

5. A different feature of a human being is exposed when he is examined from a perspective of group psychology. Since, human beings are civilized in nature, they are social beings. Therefore, this aspect of human beings should also be satisfied. They need to verify that they are not alone in their beliefs and lifestyles. They need to be convinced with the notion of "there are so many proofs that support my faith." Take a look at these people who have come from four corners of the world. People of different races, different colors, different ranks, all wearing the *ihram* (white garment) as they share the same faith, recite the same words, and stand before Ka'ba in total submission and tranquility... All of these acts support the social aspect of our lives as Muslims. Our faith is not restricted to our own individual evidence, but it gains strength and grows as big as the number of pilgrims that come to perform Hajj. This is why people who discover the mystery of group psychology come together to serve their ideologies through meetings and protests. They wish to confirm their beliefs and display their loyalty to their cause. If this is the case even in false ideologies, imagine how it should be performed for the true cause. Islam thinks about all aspects of humanity, so it suggests that the daily prayers should also be performed with a congregation. It obligates Muslims to come together at least once a week to perform the congregational Friday prayer. So the prayers are approached as unique obligations. Twice a year, during the

Eid prayers, they bring Muslims together to stand shoulder to shoulder. This practice reaches its maximum height during the Hajj.

6. The holy Qur'an states that all believers are brothers and sisters and proves this by bringing them together on an international level through the congregation of Hajj. At such a large congregation, all issues should be discussed. Conflicts and disagreements should be solved. The method of solution has been presented to us: *"If two parties of believers fall to fighting, make peace between them (and act promptly). But if one of them aggressively encroaches the rights of the other, then fight you all against the aggressive side until they comply with God's decree (concerning the matter). If they comply, then make peace between them with justice and be scrupulously equitable. Surely God loves the scrupulously equitable. The believers are but brothers, so make peace between your brothers and keep from disobedience to God in reverence for Him and piety (particularly in your duties toward one another as brothers), so that you may be shown mercy (granted a good, virtuous life in the world as individuals and as a community, and eternal happiness in the Hereafter)"* (Hujurat 49:9–10).

7. Achieving the unity of Islam and establishing strong bonds of faith among Muslims without distinguishing color, race, or nation can only be achieved through Hajj because all Muslims who come from various parts of the world will realize: Our God is One, our Lord is One, our Master is One, and our Sustainer is One... Our Prophet is one, our qiblah is one, and our religion is one...This common unity exhibits itself in thousands of ways... So many unifying qualities and so many commonalities necessitate community unity and

alliance, brotherhood and love. Indeed, all of these essentials unite Muslims and their nations like spiritual chains, just as the physical forces that keep the universe and masses together. Hajj enables the brotherhood of Islam to be experienced in a practical sense. Certainly, Hajj allows for Muslims all over the world to interact with each other on a practical platform of brotherhood with a communal feeling that instills the sense of unity in the pilgrims from different races and social, economic, and cultural backgrounds, all in their simple, two-piece garments. (It was his life-changing experience during Hajj that transformed Malcolm X, broadening his perspective with brotherhood and unity rising above the question of race).

8. Hajj also offers a practical medium through which the equality of Muslim nations is established. All Muslims, rich-poor, educated-uneducated, scholar-student, general-soldier, ruler-citizen come out of their regular clothes and wear the all-white garment. They also slip out of their ranks to become equal with their brothers so much so that they cannot be distinguished from one another. This reminds us of the white shroud wrapped around the dead body and the day of Resurrection when everyone stands up as they are.

THE UNIVERSAL ASSEMBLY OF HAJJ

The Hajj is a great annual meeting and assembly for not only the Islamic world, but also all Muslims from the four corners of the world. Now, let us analyze different aspects of the general assembly of Hajj:

1. In the 13th verse of Surah Hujurat, the Almighty God states: "*O humankind! Surely We have created you from a single*

*(pair of) male and female, and made you into tribes and families
so that you may know one another (and so build mutuality and
co-operative relationships, not so that you may take pride in your
differences of race or social rank, and breed enmities). Surely the
noblest, most honorable of you in God's sight is the one best in piety,
righteousness, and reverence for God. Surely God is All-Knowing,
All-Aware.*" In other words, I have created you in races,
tribes, and nations so that you may meet one another, establish social bonds and dealings, and support each other
through interaction. I did not create you as different tribes
and races so you may approach each other with hostility,
hatred, and violence. The "meeting" and "mutual support"
indicated in the verse may be understood in this way: An
army is divided into regiments, battalions, divisions, and pla-
toons so that each soldier is identified according to his rank,
position, and various duties, and so that each member of that
army performs a general duty under the principle rule of
mutual support to protect and defend the rights of the main
stream population. Obviously, the reason for the division is
not to compete violently against each other, develop hostility
towards the other, or to act in opposition of the other regiments. The social lives of Muslim societies are similar to that
of a huge army. This army is also divided into tribes and
nations. However, there are thousands of reasons that unite
them. Thus just as there are important reasons as to why
armies are divided into regiments, there are also important
reasons for the division of Muslim nations and countries, and
one of the main reasons is so that they could interact and
support each other. Consequently, the worship of Hajj is the

perfect occasion and medium for this general meeting and interaction.

2. Hajj also provides the opportunity for Muslims to select a powerful authority that could solve all of their spiritual and worldly problems. Through Hajj, Muslims practice working together as one organized body. Let us further investigate the issue as it appears in the Qur'an: *"You are the best of peoples, evolved for mankind, enjoining what is right, forbidding what is wrong"* (Al Imran 3:110); *"Thus, have We made of you an Ummah justly balanced, that you might be witnesses over the nations"* (Baqara 2:143); *"And fight them on until there is no more tumult or oppression"* (Baqara 2:193). The above verses are an indication that Muslims are given the duty of bringing balance to the world. Again, verses 9-10 of the Surah Hujurat indicate the same principle.

> We surely established him with power in the land, and for everything (that he rightly purposed) We granted him a way (the just means appropriate to just ends). One such way he followed, until, when he reached the setting-place of the sun, he saw it setting in a spring of hot and black muddy water, and nearby he found a people. We said: "O Dhu'l-Qarnayn! You can either punish them or you can treat them with kindness. (Which way will you choose?)" He said: "As for him who does wrong (by disbelieving in Him or associating partners with Him and oppressing others) we will punish him and then he is brought back to his Lord, and He punishes him in an indescribable manner. But as for him who believes and does good, righteous deeds, for him the recompense of the best is due, and we will speak to him an easy word of Our command (we will charge him with easy tasks)." Then he followed another

way, until, when he reached the rising-place of the sun and found it rising on a people for whom We had provided no shelter against it. So it was (such was their state and the extent of Dhu'l-Qarnayn's power). We assuredly encompassed all concerning him in Our Knowledge. Then he followed another way, until, when he reached (a place) between two mountain-barriers, he found before them a people who scarcely understood a word. They said: "O Dhu'l-Qarnayn! Gog and Magog are causing disorder in this land. May we pay you a tribute so that you set a barrier between us and them?" He said: "What my Lord has established me in (the power that He has granted me on this earth) is better (than what you offer). So help me with strength (manpower) and I will set a strong rampart between you and them. "Bring me blocks of iron." Then, after he had filled up (the space between) the two steep mountain-sides, he said: "(Light a fire and) work your bellows!" At length, when he had made it (glow red like) fire, he said: "Bring me molten copper that I may pour upon it." And they (Gog and Magog) were no longer able to surmount, nor were they able to dig their way through (the barrier). (Kahf 18:84–97)

These verses indicate that Muslims need to make an effort to obtain power so that they could bring justice and peace to the world.

In order to spread the exalted name of God to the world, besides strengthening their faith and morals, Muslims also need to advance in material power. Just like Dhu'l-Qarnayn, Muslims must be equipped with both spiritual and material power. The objective is not to colonize the world and make slaves out of fellow human beings. On the contrary, it is initially to protect one's own nation and then to rush to the aid of all Muslims and non-Muslims who are being oppressed or exploited no matter to which race or ethnicity they belong. The aim is to protect the rights of the entire humanity and to bring balance to the world. Placing human beings under the protection of Islam will also open and soften their hearts towards Islam. Dhu'l-Qarnayn, who protected the innocent from the tyranny and despotism of the Gog and Magog by constructing a great wall, did not even request a payment for his efforts; therefore, he serves as a great example for us. To achieve such an important objective, Muslims who gather each year during the Hajj season should consult one another and join forces both spiritually and materially only to please God. The worship of Hajj is the best medium for this. The conscience of the Islamic world that is currently at a blooming stage will yield beautiful fruits in the near future. India and Pakistan are the capable sons of Islam who are currently at an educational stage; Egypt is the intelligent child of Islam; Turkistan and the Caucasus are the two courageous sons of Islam. Once these noble sons receive their testimonies, they will lead a continent and wave the banner of their father, Islam, and its justice against all odds as they follow their divine destiny and declare the infinite purpose of humanity.

3. For Muslims, Hajj is an academy. This academy teaches patience and exertion. The academy of Hajj trains its pupils to abstain from the desires of the flesh and to behave in kindness and munificence towards their brothers. This pilgrimage also teaches one to spend without expecting anything in return and enhances the feeling of giving everything for the sake of God. The good and the bad are

symbolized during Hajj and presented before the eyes of all believers as enemies or friends of God. The profound meanings of certain practices such as the stoning of the Satan, tawaf around Ka'ba, salutation of Hajar al-Aswad, and visiting Medina will be embroidered into the hearts, minds, and inner worlds of Muslims.

4. Through Hajj, many beautiful feelings and emotions will be rejuvenated in the hearts of Muslims. The memories and reminiscences of the early Muslims who were mesmerized by the Qur'anic revelations and lived as living Qur'ans on this land will reappear in the minds and hearts of the pilgrims, who will then become examples of their reflections.

5. The spreading of modern science is based on constant interaction between the nations, desire for knowledge, and mutual support between the disciplines. If we had utilized the congregation of Hajj to spread the wisdom of our chemists who had established the fundamental substances of modern chemistry, such as nitric acids, and the knowledge of our physicists who had proposed the fundamentals of motion and force, and the magnificent intellect of Muhammad al-Khwarizmi Al-Jabir, who discovered algebra (The term "algebra" is derived from the Arabic *al-jabr* in the title of his *Al-Jabr*), the stepping stone of modern civilizations at a time when other nations were still living in the stone ages, we would have been building spaceships. Unfortunately, we have not benefitted from the profound meaning and deep mystery that the Hajj offers to Muslims. In reality, both modern science and religious doctrine should have been spread to the world of Islam through the practice of Hajj.

6. In the field of international trade, issues such as power to purchase, conditions of distribution, commercial needs rising from different lifestyles and weather conditions, collective firms and agencies that operate on an international level, cost standards according to labor, the guarantee of obtaining the cheapest fees for raw and processed materials, and various other trade principles based on Islamic brotherhood could have easily been established through Hajj. The common market that the European Union has been concentrating on will bring enormous profits in the future. These amazing principles were prescribed by Islam through Hajj many centuries ago.

7. "Travel and you shall find health" is a hadith qudsi that suggests journeys such as the pilgrimage performed during Hajj provides an opportunity for recovery from many spiritual and physical illnesses. The mistakes and errors made by the people of many nations, wicked traditions and customs, unhealthy family lifestyles, and the lack of sacrifice in social life can be corrected or improved through the friendships established with other people coming from different parts of the world. The adventures of Malcolm X, who followed a path that contradicted the principles of *Ahl as-Sunnah wa'l-Jama'ah* (main body of the Muslim Community) prior to Hajj, is a great example. Certainly, the general depression experienced by the world of Islam today originates from the lack of communication and interaction that the Hajj offers. In this regard, the responsibility of both spiritual and governmental leaders of the Islamic nations is enormous.

It is a possibility that an Islamic nation may be invaded and oppressed by non-Muslims. And the people of this nation may not have the means to defend themselves. In such a situation, the institute of Hajj should become a place where all Muslim brothers think as one great brain to find a solution to protect their brothers who are in distress.

In the aforementioned dream in which Muslims were punished with various disasters and calamities for refraining from zakat, fasting, and prayers, Hajj was not mentioned. The reason for this is explained as follows: "the dream was silenced at Hajj," because abandoning Hajj and its practices did not cause a regular disaster but rather attracted the wrath of God! (Disasters are ransoms paid for sins, but the wrath of God is different). So when the wrath of God comes down as punishment, it does not compensate for sins. On the contrary, sins are increased.

Abandoning the practice of Hajj is also abandoning one of Islam's greatest principles and political implementations that enable Muslims to meet, interact, and support each other. Therefore, this also allows the enemies of Islam how to utilize this disunity against Muslims:

- Take a look at India, it has murdered its father assuming that he was the enemy and now, it sits by his side and weeps.

- Look at the Tatars and Caucasus, they do not even realize that the person they have helped murder is their mother...now there are crying in vain.

- Take a look at the Arabs, they have killed their gallant brother by mistake...now, they are so confused that they cannot even weep.

- Here is Africa; they slaughtered their sibling...now they are screaming in despair.

- The world of Islam stands before us...through somnolence they have killed their son who carried the banner...now they mourn the death of their child like a sobbing mother.
- Indeed, many Muslims who abandoned the blessed journey of Hajj, have walked through many journeys under the banner of the enemy...learn a lesson.

DECLARATION OF SERVANTHOOD BY THE MUSLIM COMMUNITY

One of the many beautiful aspects of servanthood is that the noble Messenger of God brings the hearts of believers together during the Eid, Friday, and congregational prayers. He unites their tongues in one word. This is so significant that the human beings respond to the exalted announcement of the Almighty God with recitations echoing from their hearts and tongues.

Those recitations, prayers, and remembrance support one another in such a harmonious universal way that they manifest a grand servanthood before the Omnipotence of the Eternal Lord; it is as if the entire planet earth has joined the recitation. It prays as it revolves. And with objects around it, the planet earth submits to the commandment that comes from beyond the boundaries of the universe, *"Perform the prayer steadfastly"* (Baqara 2:43). With this mysterious unity, the human being, who is a weak creature, like an atom in comparison to the universe, becomes the beloved servant of the Creator of the universe and the earth, a caliph or a sultan of the world, leader of the animal kingdom, and the purpose and result of creation due to the enormity of his servanthood.

Yes, the chanting of millions of believers who scream out, "Allahu Akbar" during the prayers unites in the realm of the unseen; if this chant united in this world also, the entire planet would transform into a gigantic human being who would shout the words "Allahu Akbar!" Making the intention with its heart—the Ka'ba—the earth then experiences great tremors as the world of Islam unites with recitations and prayers and utters the words "Allahu Akbar!" during the congregational prayer, in particular during the Eid prayer. Just as the uttering of a single "Allahu Akbar" produces countless echoes, so too acceptable recitations and glorifications of believers echo through the universe like waves that reach all the way to the realm of Barzakh, where the souls of the deceased will rest until the Day of Resurrection.

It is amazing to behold millions of pilgrims performing their Eid prayer in congregation around the Ka'ba. Indeed, one would observe with his imagination the rings that constantly grow around Ka'ba, just like a rose-flower, as they begin with the first line of performers that stand closest to Ka'ba and the furthest line of ring that represents the entire world of Islam. In this way, the entire Muslim community all over the world stands for the prayer in rows forming great rings around the Ka'ba like the layers of petals around the tiny black tassels. Just like the rose-flower with black tassels at its center, the rose city, mother of cities, and belly button of the world is Mecca, and the Ka'ba is its center with its black cloth. One ring after another, the entire world lines up forming great rings around it, and the daily prayers never stop around the world.

The beautiful picture of this astounding congregation that stands in perfect lines as they decorate the great mosque of the earth with their movements is photographed with divine cameras and preserved in the pages of the realm of *Mithal*, or Representations, where meanings or abstract truths are reflected and represented. (The reflections in this realm of *Mithal* are called "the ideal or reflected forms"). Every Muslim should include himself into these lines and into this amazing congregation so that each word he utters during the prayer becomes solid evidence with the support and confirmation of the entire body of believers. For example, when a Muslim says "Alhamdulillah" (All praise be to God) during the prayer, it is as if all Muslims who make up this great congregation reply with the words, "You have spoken the truth!" and confirm his declaration. As a result, their confirmations act as a spiritual shield that protects and defends him from suspicions and trepidations. At the same time, all of his emotional faculties and feelings receive their share out of that particular prayer.

INDEX

A

ablution (*wudu'*), 21, 29, 58-60, 62-67, 70, 72-73, 100; significance of, 59

Abraham (Prophet), 37, 146-148

Abu Bakr, 134

Abu Darda, 64

Abu Hurayra, 84, 135

Africa, 74, 158

Ahl as-Sunnah wa'l-Jama'ah, 88, 157

Aisha bint Abu Bakr, 13

alcohol, 12-14, 16, 96, 118; abuse, 16; prohibition, 12, 14

alcoholism, 13, 16; treatments for, 13

algebra, 156

Alhamdulillah, 26-28, 161

Ali ibn Abi Talib, 60

Allahu Akbar, 26-29, 146, 160

Altug, Timucin, 20

American, 15-16

anarchism, 135

Arab, 72, 158

Arabian Peninsula, 60, 148

arrogance, 40, 48-49, 120, 131, 141, 144

arteriosclerosis, 100, 123-125

Ascension, the, 6-7, 39

astral double, 72

Ayatu'l-Kursiyy, 111

B

Babuna, Cevat, 81

bacteria, 58-59, 61-63, 65-66, 73-75, 138; as the biggest nemesis of teeth, 73; discovery of, 59

balance; of acids, bases and salts, 90

Battle of Trench, 88

Beard, Rebecca, 56

Beautiful Names of God, 4-5, 50; Allah, 26-28, 106, 135-136, 148; All-Aware, 152; All-Beauteous, 33, 36; All-Clement, 142; All-Compassionate, 33, 36, 38-39, 42; All-Embracing, 142-143; All-Generous, 38; All-Glorious, 32, 36, 39; All-Great, 26-29, 39, 48, 146; All-Knowing, 128, 142-143, 152; All-Merciful, 31-32, 37, 39; All-Powerful, 26, 33, 36, 38, 119; All-Wealthy, 142; All-Wise, 37, 60, 87-88, 128; Divine Beauty, 4, 35, 37, 39; Beauty of Divine Essence, 35; Changer of Night and Day, 36; Creator,